NINE SCROLLS OF ESSENTIAL WISDOM

From the book...

ESSENTIAL WISDOM

Personal Development and Soul Transformation

Concept and Produced by Dave Gould

Nine Scrolls of Essential Wisdom
Copyright © 2016 by Essential Wisdom, LLC
All rights reserved worldwide.

No part of this book may be reproduced, redistributed, transmitted, retransmitted, translated, sold, given away, decompiled or otherwise circumvented by any means, electronic or mechanical, including photocopying, recording, or by any information storage or retrieval system, without written permission from the Essential Wisdom, LLC.

This book is designed to provide information and processes used by the contributing authors. Every effort has been made to make it as complete and accurate as possible, but no warranty is implied.

Editorial Direction: Bernice Angoh
Editors: Dave Gould, Bernice Angoh, and Candy Zulkosky

Cover Layout and Design : Dave Gould

Layout and Design by James Woosley, FreeAgentPress.com

Nine Essential Wisdom Scrolls. / Essential Wisdom, LLC,

www.essentialwisdom.com

SBN-10:1-944913-11-4
ISBN-13:978-1-944913-11-3.

INTRODUCTION
Essential Wisdom

Dear Reader,

    We are very pleased to have you as part of the *Essential Wisdom* family as an early adopter and foundational member.

    This mini book was created just for you; to show our appreciation while giving you a glimpse into the wealth of knowledge that is synonymous with *Essential Wisdom*. In this book you'll find nine of the thirty-three chapters from our book, *Essential Wisdom: Personal Development and Soul Transformation*. In some of the chapters you may find the name 'Lucas Hamilton' mentioned. Bear in mind, Lucas's story IS NOT a part of this mini book but is included in the full version of the book, complete with all thirty-three chapters. You are in for the ride of your life as Lucas takes you on an incredible journey of awakening and transformation.

    Our hope is that you find within these pages, the very truth that sings inside of your heart and soul. Thank you, once again, for coming on this incredible journey with us, we promise to thrill you but even more so, we are honored by your acceptance of us, to dwell in the beauty of your heart.

> *Essential Wisdom is a comprehensive collection of progressive ideas that inspire and challenge our readers to "awaken" to their true individual potentials. Previously unforeseen possibilities become visible as the wisdom in the book helps readers to see the world through a new lens. This newfound self-awareness awakens a shift across the different areas of the reader's human life.*
>
> **–Essential Wisdom Synopsis**

Lucas Hamilton will walk each step of this journey with the reader, helping to define the path, the pitfalls, and the joys. As each of these 36 chapters unfold, the reader finds that their own personal journey is made more real and transformational through experiencing the simultaneous journal of our fictional story and character of Lucas Hamilton.

> *Who is Lucas Hamilton? Spoiled and entitled, wants nothing but to escape the life he'd been living for twenty-one years. He is certain that, being his grandfather's favorite and his workaholic dad's burden, the inheritance from his grandfather's will is his only ticket out. He wants to live life on his own terms, wild, reckless, and indulgent. But all his plans come to a halt when he is left an envelope instead of money from the will. ...With nothing more to lose, he decides to follow the instructions his late grandfather left. Suddenly, the big brown manila envelope he inherited held more hope for him than he'd ever care to admit.*
>
> **–Essential Wisdom Synopsis**

Here are nine chapters to get you excited:

1. It's a new beginning with *Your Awakening—a New Beginning*.

2. Rejoice in the *Universal Law of Love—The Awakened Self* as shared by Wanda Krause.

3. Understand gratitude in a completely different light as experienced and explained by Bernice Angoh in *Gratitude—the Birth of Happiness*.

4. Join Dave Elliot to embrace the essential secrets for getting and staying engaged in a life-long partnership in *Marriage—Creating an Awakened Legendary Relationship*.

5. Dealing with the end of a relationship. Jim Rogers shares *Nothing Lasts Forever—How the Awakened Mind Handles the Transition to Being Single*.

6. Awaken into self-awareness with the wisdom of Dr. Nic Lucas in *Choose to Step into Your Greatness*.

7. Recognize the symbiosis between stress and life-balance with Penny Zenker in *The Heart of Productivity*.

8. Understand your answer to the question, Who Am I with Shajen Joy Aziz in *Self-Actualization—Your Spiritual Spunk*.

9. Get emotional and focused on what happiness means to you in the *Happiness Formula—Journey of a Life Well-Lived* by Gary King.

1
YOUR AWAKENING
A New Beginning

A time comes in your life when you finally get it. When, in the midst of all your fears and insanity, you stop dead in your tracks and somewhere the voice inside your head cries out, ENOUGH! Enough fighting and crying and blaming and struggling to hold on. Then, like a child quieting down after a tantrum, you blink back your tears and begin to look at the world through new eyes.

This is your awakening.

You realize it's time to stop hoping and waiting for something to change, or for happiness, safety and security to magically appear over the next horizon.

You realize that in the real world there aren't always fairy tale endings, and that any guarantee of "happily ever after" must begin with you, and in the process a sense of serenity is born of acceptance.

You awaken to the fact that you are not perfect and that not everyone will always love, appreciate or approve of who or what you are, and that's OK. They are entitled to their own views and opinions.

You learn the importance of loving and championing yourself, and in the process a sense of new found confidence is born of self-approval.

Your stop complaining and blaming other people for the things they did to you–or didn't do for you–and you learn that the only thing you can really count on is the unexpected.

You learn that people don't always say what they mean or mean what they say and that not everyone will always be there for you and everything isn't always about you.

So, you learn to stand on your own and to take care of yourself, and in the process a sense of safety and security is born of self-reliance.

You stop judging and pointing fingers and you begin to accept people as they are and to overlook their shortcomings and human frailties, and in the process a sense of peace and contentment is born of forgiveness.

You learn to open up to new worlds and different points of view. You begin reassessing and redefining who you are and what you really stand for.

You learn the difference between wanting and needing and you begin to discard the doctrines and values you've outgrown, or should never have bought into to begin with.

1 | Your Awakening

You learn that there is power and glory in creating and contributing and you stop maneuvering through life merely as a "consumer" looking for you next fix.

You learn that principles such as honesty and integrity are not the outdated ideals of a bygone era, but the mortar that holds together the foundation upon which you must build a life.

You learn that you don't know everything, it's not your job to save the world and that you can't teach a pig to sing. You learn the only cross to bear is the one you choose to carry and that martyrs get burned at the stake.

Then you learn about love. You learn to look at relationships as they really are and not as you would have them be. You learn that alone does not mean lonely.

You stop trying to control people, situations and outcomes. You learn to distinguish between guilt and responsibility and the importance of setting boundaries and learning to say NO.

You also stop working so hard at putting your feelings aside, smoothing things over and ignoring your needs.

You learn that your body really is your temple. You begin to care for it and treat it with respect. You begin to eat a balanced diet, drinking more water, and take more time to exercise.

You learn that being tired fuels doubt, fear, and uncertainty and so you take more time to rest. And, just food fuels the body, laughter fuels our soul. So you take more time to laugh and to play.

You learn that, for the most part, you get in life what you deserve, and that much of life truly is a self-fulfilling prophecy.

You learn that anything worth achieving is worth working for and that wishing for something to happen be different than working toward making it happen.

More importantly, you learn that in order to achieve success you need direction, discipline and perseverance. You learn that no one can do it all alone, and that it's OK to risk asking for help.

You learn the only thing you must truly fear is fear itself. You learn to step right into and through your fears because you know that whatever happens you can handle it and to give in to fear is to give away the right to live life on your own terms.

You learn to fight for your life and not to squander it living under a cloud of impending doom.

You learn that life isn't always fair, you don't always get what you think you deserve and that sometimes bad things happen to unsuspecting, good people, and you learn not to always take it personally.

You learn that nobody's punishing you and everything isn't always somebody's fault. It's just life happening. You learn to admit when you are wrong and to build bridges instead of walls.

You lean that negative feelings such as anger, envy and resentment must be understood and redirected or they will suffocate the life out of you and poison the universe that surrounds you.

You learn to be thankful and to take comfort in many of the simple things we take for granted, things that millions of people upon the earth can only dream about: a full refrigerator, clean running water, a soft warm bed, a long hot shower.

Then, you begin to take responsibility for yourself by yourself and you make yourself a promise to never betray yourself and to never, ever settle for less than your heart's desire.

You make it a point to keep smiling, to keep trusting, and to stay open to every wonderful possibility.

You hang a wind chime outside your window so you can listen to the wind.

Finally, with courage in your heart, you take a stand, you take a deep breath, and you begin to design the life you want to live as best as you can.

Now is the time for you to change your mindset. Let go of limiting beliefs and become the person you were always meant to be. I believe in you, I really do. Find your passion, my friend. Think big.

Shoot for the stars. This is what the rest of your life is going to be. You have no time left to dilly dally, to wander aimlessly through the years.

It's rather simple–boils down to a choice–chose to make that choice today; to rise up and step into your greatness!

2
UNIVERSAL LAW OF LOVE

The Awakened Self

Dr. Wanda Krause

With the passing of our beloved dog recently, we are shown one way in which we have been blessed with love. She reminded us to play often; she offered comfort, protection, companionship, licks and kisses. We gave protection, hugs, tons of kisses, treats. Countless interactions with her were imbued with love. And now we yearn to feel her by holding her toy and imagine she is playfully running alongside us. Our yearning is for this particular experience of love with which we were so sweetly blessed. Indeed, love takes forms. And so, love is and will be felt, experienced as lost, and found again in a multitude of forms, each having their own unique vibration of it. This experience teaches us again that life is really about receiving love and giving love, in fact, being love.

Love birthed you. Every act of creation happens with love and from love. Love is The Source of everything manifested. It is The Highest of vibrations in the universe moving through matter so we experience It. In this lies one of the most precious keys for navigating life. Embrace and live the life you have to the fullest, allow yourself to overflow with love, allow yourself to be guided by It and use It with purpose and intent. In the most joy-filled moments, love envelopes you in a sensation, being and realization that life is to, in fact, be enjoyed. It also pierces through the darkest and deepest abyss we might find ourselves. It kindles a light within the heart that is tangible and real. In the most crushing moments, love kindles the spark of hope one needs, a kind of reassurance, a greater awareness, indeed, a realization that from the pain, from the ashes there is also its essence to be experienced–an All-Knowing Love.

Khalil Gibran tells,

> "When love beckons to you follow him, though his ways are hard and steep. And when his wings enfold you yield to him, though the sword hidden among his pinions may wound you. And when he speaks to you believe in him, though his voice may shatter your dreams as the north wind lays waste the garden. For even as love crowns you so shall he crucify you. Even as he is for your growth so is he for your pruning. Even as he ascends to your height and caresses your tenderest branches that quiver in the sun, so shall he descend to your roots and shake them in their clinging to the earth. Like sheaves of corn he gathers you unto himself. He threshes you to make you naked. He sifts you to free you from your husks. He grinds you to whiteness. He kneads you until you are pliant; and then he

assigns you to his sacred fire, that you may become sacred bread for God's sacred feast. All these things shall love do unto you that you may know the secrets of your heart, and in that knowledge become a fragment of Life's heart."

Love is a mercy that is offered through those moments of pain, the Higher vibration that pierces through. If we allow, love can be invited in, in the belief–if not the realization–that there is purpose and, even if we do not fully comprehend, that there is Mercy in that purpose. Love is the embracing of the higher Wisdom, the All Wise, indeed, more than embracing but submitting. It is the process of opening our hearts in spite of the pain felt in rejection, belligerent actions of others, life's trials and love itself.

Love is an act. The first part of that act is choosing love. You allow love to manifest and do its work by opening, embracing and submitting to it; and by allowing, enabling, exercising and facilitating it into our lives and the lives of others. But what if others are not receptive to love? What of people resistant to our extension of our love? Enemies, a neighbor, a lover? Love is in the act of extending ourselves to others, especially when we have all logical reason to shut down. Love is not just a feeling that spontaneously happens between two people or what you feel for something that brings you joy. It is something we help birth. We make love happen. We open, bring it in and direct it. If more of us could only know. Love is the most powerful Source in the universe, and that we can actually learn to use and work–co-create–with It.

Hence, as love is not just a force but an act, it will remain elusive if we chase it. As Jalal ad-Din Rumi reminds, *"Your task is not to seek for love, but merely to seek and find all the barriers within yourself that you have built against it."* Living and experiencing more love in our lives comes about through the cracking open of our hearts, embracing our darkness, taking responsibility where needed, and letting out light to heal ourselves and heal others. This is the process of freeing ourselves from the barriers to our own love that is the key to live life fully.

The law of love states that you experience love by giving love. You have love in your life when you give it freely, when there are no strings attached, and when you continue to love even when you do not see love returned to you. But it will return to you, if not from the person you are giving love to, from someone else. Bottom line, you must receive what you give. If you want love, give love! It will most often be through the small things that require us to truly give of ourselves and truly put us to the test of loving, such as in the home where no one can glorify valiant acts or with trying neighbors. The great religions tell us to: *"Love your neighbor as you love yourself" – Saint Paul, Galatians 5:14*, and there is great wisdom to be gained in this.

Hadia El-Attar, a woman who has been through so many trials herself, including as a child losing her mother in an assassination attempt on her father, a political figure, and then losing her daughter to a car accident, taught me an incredible lesson about love. Her lesson and example is with a new neighbor, someone she had never met before and someone who could offer her nothing. When Hadia greeted her for the first few times, the neighbor simply looked down or looked the other way. After this first week, Hadia could have chosen to look the other way in the mornings too. Such reciprocity would be logical. Few would do otherwise. Instead, Hadia made a choice to continue a simple expression of love. Hadia saw her neighbor virtually every morning as the two stepped out about the same time to head to work and Hadia mustered the courage to say a pleasant "good morning" greeting. Hadia explained that being consistent with this gesture, of course, took resolve, intent and will. For literally a whole year, she persisted in providing her neighbor this tiny act of love. It was a full year later that one morning the woman stopped in front of Hadia and burst out in tears. Hadia told me this woman looked into her eyes for the first time. What she told Hadia shows the impact of persistent and disciplined acts of love. She told Hadia that Hadia was the only friend she had, and that she was going to be admitted into a psychiatric hospital the following day. In fact, she profusely thanked Hadia for being her friend.

The feeling and the experience of love is the side-product of love as a deed. Love is a deed in doing the "act"–what it takes to create that experience of it. Herein is the wisdom as there will be so many situations and issues we will not want to have to deal with. In many respects, we experience those very situations we least want. Those are, however, the opportunities in which we are invited to extend love. The opening to receive and give in these situations is what we need to do. The process of giving love is not merely for the receiver. There is a growing into greater awareness that happens when we discipline ourselves to give, when we practice opening and submitting to love's force. The whole process is transformational and being at the center of the process, we ourselves are the ones that are really truly benefitting from the love we are opening to receive and extend. It is, therefore, not about the one we are extending love to, although touching the lives of others is the process for evolution. It is us – the doers, the actors–in the theater of receiving and giving love that in the process find meaning and purpose, indeed our essence. Our meaning and purpose is a return to that which birthed us, our essence.

Love is the most political tool we have to work with and co-create with in this world. It is the consciousness that Einstein spoke about when he said *"We can't solve problems by using the same kind of thinking we used when we created them."* He was not speaking merely of the faculty of intelligence we have coupled with his words or discoveries. It is not the mind we need to create peace, stronger communities, closer families and better selves. It is the mind of the heart.

It is love. Hadia El-Attar chose to rise in consciousness, not solving the situation with the same type of thinking that created it. The rise in consciousness was expressed with a simple gesture of a greeting that touched her neighbor profoundly. If we can learn to implement such consistent and disciplined acts of love, no matter how difficult our own burdens are, we won't only impact our neighborhoods, but contribute to making the world a profoundly more loving place. World peace depends on our ability to express a higher consciousness through simple acts of love, consistently.

Make love a choice. Every morning choose love. Place yourself in the vibration of love by giving thanks for all the forms of love you experience. You can start by giving gratitude for a few things. If you are finding yourself in the midst of a painful reality right now, you may wish you didn't have to deal with it or have it happen to you. But, I ask you to not resist it. In the heart of it is love. Seek to embrace all of it. Don't intellectualize it. Rather, submit to it. You will move much quicker to the gift it has in its offering. Gift yourself forgiveness, where needed. Be kind to yourself. Gift yourself love by making room for you this day. Give yourself a candle-lit bath, a walk in nature, five minutes smelling flowers in a flower shop, playtime with a pet, time with a sport activity you enjoy, read uplifting literature, something loving. Part of receiving love could entail asking your partner for a massage. Set aside time for loving activities for you twice a day and be militant about your gifts to you. You simply cannot give if your cup is empty.

Intend love in what you do throughout your day. If prayer is part of your morning routine, ask that you be an instrument of love to bringing It whomever and wherever is needed during your day. During your day be present to situations where love is needed. In trying situations affirm, "I am love." As Mother Teresa tells us, "It's not how much we give but how much love we put into giving." Take your love to the little things, first, into the mundane. Then into the places and to the people no one out there will ever know about, and also to the people and things who will never be able to repay you. Every day.

Learning where boundaries lie in love is critical to being the vessel through which love can flow continuously. If the walls of your vessel have holes, you cannot direct love effectively and hold as much love or give love endlessly. If you have no walls, you are soon an empty cup. Giving love unconditionally does not mean you do not discriminate. While you give love without requiring another to change, if that other seeks to tear you down and does not cease, you will have to choose to love from afar. Do not justify putting yourself in a position to be weakened, cut down and dehumanized for the sake of another or for the sake of any notion of even love itself. Such an act is not nurturing to anyone. Chipping away at another's walls, whether a partner's, a parent's, a child's, a neighbor's or a whole nation's, through forgiveness, compassion and giving can lead to transformation, peace and harmony. But you will also need to assess whether to act with love from afar, where self-preservation is love, or closely, where vulnerability and sacrifice is love. The bottom line is that you remain the vessel to give love.

From Hadia's example, we can see also how the law of harvest works. Similar to the Chinese bamboo tree, when you give and give, not for the person or any other reason but because love itself and doing the act of love is your purpose, the seed you planted and watered consistently with love may take long to see but it must sprout! You cannot see the bamboo plant's roots growing under the soil. You wait but still see nothing. Most will tell you to give up when months later there is no proof to show for all your waiting and nurturing. But, in the case of the bamboo, you nurture it by watering it consistently.

Few people will support your relentless acts of love because still few are at a higher conscious understanding of love. This is your task, to lead the submission, embrace and expression of it, patiently and consistently.

The bamboo tree takes between five and eight years to sprout above the soil. Your task may take an entire year; it may take longer. If your mission is world peace, it may take 500 years, as former American ambassador, policy advisor to Richard Nixon and deputy director of the National Security Council, Dr. Robert D. Crane, once told me. You will not see the roots growing. In fact, be prepared to experience what might appear to be "death," an ending or some undesired result to what you have nurtured. But, one day, and often it is sudden, your acts of love will manifest into its own magnificence, of which you are a part. You need know only this; leave the timing or the forms as results, themselves, to the All-Knowing Love. Embracing, indeed, submitting to love and expressing it is stepping into a higher consciousness, that of the ultimate power, beauty and truth, as it desires to enfold and unfold through us.

> *"Yesterday we obeyed kings and bent our necks before emperors. But today we kneel only to truth, Follow only beauty, And obey only love."*
>
> **–Khalil Gibran**

3
GRATITUDE

The Birth of Happiness

Bernice Angoh

The Rebel, the Gatekeeper, the Creator, & the Healer

The awakened mind views gratitude much differently than the mind which is not: one merely lists and counts the things they are grateful for as though it were some magical spell to conjure up more things for their satisfaction, while the other becomes and lives gratitude due to a deep awareness of them being the source from which all things come to life.

Gratitude is defined as an expression of appreciation or having a great attitude in whatever situation one is faced with. As with most things in life, there are always different views and different perspectives to the same truth: gratitude is the sunlight needed for all flowers of virtue. Gratitude is more than just a virtue, she is the above and below, the earth and the sun that gives all virtues (flowers) their shining qualities (colors).

Life as we know it would cease to exist were it not for this nine-lettered word which, ironically, is a very symbolic number in many different ancient cultures.

Before we talk about the different levels and attributes of gratitude let's take a moment to see what a few different cultures say about it.

Thank You

In India it is not necessary to say 'thank you' or 'Shukriya' to friends and family because they believe friends and family are expected to be there for one another. They truly embrace the phrase 'family is everything'. Being there for those you love is their way to express gratitude and needs no recognition.

The Chinese favor gestures over words. Saying 'thank you' is easily one of the quickest ways to create a barrier between you and the people around you; instead it is encouraged to lose the formality and show genuine gratitude by action. The Chinese see the Westerner's overly expressed gratitude for every little thing to be insincere. Their system of 'bao' is more of a collective than an individualistic approach to showing and expressing gratitude; what you do, you do not just for yourself but for many involved. 'Bao' literally means 'reciprocity'; that each act of kindness springs a debt of favorable kindness that will be returned to you in life.

If you want to show gratitude, you will really have to 'show' what you are doing for your society and how you are growing individually by building great relationships with others. It is not necessary to just say 'thank you' or 'xiexie', let your action have an impact.

The Mayans had a daily prayer of gratitude which they performed upon waking up. They acknowledged the seven directions of north, south, east, west, up, down and center. They believed in the blessings from nature and so they would ask permission to access the gifts that are coming to them. They asked the earth permission before ploughing the soil to plant in it, permission from a plant before harvesting it and permission from water before using it to bathe.

In ancient Kemet, where humanity's quest for closeness with the divine began, the importance of honoring the ancestral spirit was highly observed and revered. It was a way of showing gratitude for those through whom we came to be and for who we'd become through the values they left behind. Personal hygiene, according to them, was very important because it directly affected spiritual cleanliness, without which it was believed no interaction with the spiritual world was possible. Showing gratitude was considered a contribution; a contribution in honoring the planet and each other by always being mindful of our deeds, words and thoughts.

The Different Levels of Gratitude

As with the five stages of grieving, there are four horizontal levels of gratitude and attributes that are characteristic with of an awakened mind.

"The Highest tribute to the dead is not grief but gratitude."

–Thornton Wilder

The Rebel

It is almost impossible to feel grateful when someone you love has just passed away, when your heart is broken and when you're starving or homeless. How can you be grateful in those times when all you want to do is take out your bleeding heart and throw it across the room? Gratitude is as fleeting as the wind in moments like these. Gratitude was never meant to be an antidote nor a placebo. Gratitude is a rebel.

In times of pain and sorrow, in moments of doubts and fear, our hearts and minds seldom move towards being grateful. When things aren't going the way we planned, thought or expected, we sometimes become very self-involved. The irony is that gratitude works the same way, except the self is extended outward. It doesn't wallow in self-pity, blame or shame, it rebels against those.

Gratitude is a rebel. It shows up defiantly in tough times, and brings with it a legion of friends to reward the rebel. The rebel is the mother of strength and courage.

It is very important to grieve and allow the emotions to pass through us; in the African culture, tears are a necessary part of cleansing any negative emotions and energies within the body. The rebelliousness of gratitude is refusing to stay in that state, and instead, choosing to rise out and above it; the recognition that you've suffered enough and must find a way to live with or without the pain.

The rebel finds a way to not only survive but to thrive; to be like the rose with all its thorns still in place, not as a show of pity but as a show of pride of having accomplished the hardest; to shine in spite of. The rebel does not hide his/her battle scars; they are just a beautiful reminder that every great win is preceded by a great battle. The rebel finds within the dark, the glittering stars that shine, a reminder of those precious moments that make the heart warm against the nightfall of cold and darkness. The rebel says 'I AM' still here and I accept this journey and all its surprises.

It is at this moment that the next flower of gratitude sprouts; the Healer who is the mother of peace.

"When you practice gratefulness, there is a sense of respect towards others."

–Dalai Lama

The Healer

To be grateful is to be pregnant with the fullness of NOW. Gratitude draws our attention away from worries, anxiety, depression and uncertainties and brings us to a place of peace. To be grateful is to be in tune with the life force of life and like a skill, it can be practiced until we not only see it as a thing to do or a way to be but most importantly, a constant breath.

The very essence of being grateful is life. Gratitude is acknowledging those free gifts that come to you with barely or no effort on your part; like breathing. Breathing in oxygen allows for our human bodies to function properly and work like it ought. Without oxygen our organs shut down and we become diseased and slowly pass away. Gratitude is much like oxygen in that it allows for all those positive elements of joy, happiness, contentment and peace to flow and energize our being to the point that we want to share it with others.

"No act of kindness, no matter how small, is ever wasted."

–Aesop's Fables 'The Lion and the Mouse'

To heal yourself is to heal the world. To be at peace with yourself is to be at peace with the world. Whatever we are, the world becomes, not as an instantaneous process but as a ripple in addition to the waves in a body of water moving towards the shore.

"Neither rejoice nor lament prematurely, for whatever may happen, all will be well if we only have health; for happiness exists-merely in the imagination."

–Wolfgang Amadeus Mozart

Present in the healer is also the rebel who has gone through his/her own share of experiences and can now comfort, listen and be there for another. The healer has finally come to one of the secrets knowing that all is well, and all will pass. It is not just passing through the storm, but allowing the storm to pass through you to shake all the ripe 'fruits' down and moving the right things into their right places. The healer knows that healing comes only after a hurt, and also that there are no healers without scars of overcoming. The best healers have been healed. For the awakened mind, gratitude is the very important score in every motion picture, reminding us that we can carry all the heavy, and even sing through it all. The healer, who is the mother of peace, is also the beholder of all the puzzle pieces she hands to the gatekeeper.

"Gratitude is not only the greatest of all virtues, but the parent of all others."

–Marcus Tullius Cicero

> *"If awareness is the door to an abundant life, then gratitude is the gatekeeper who holds the key."*
>
> –Bernice Angoh

The Gatekeeper

Being grateful and practicing gratitude is a sure way to stand before every door of this magnificent swirl called life and to know that one door is not better than the other, that all doors are full of possibilities because your attitude decides which room or world lies beyond. You don't go in looking for what to find, you bring with you what to 'decorate' your world with. The gatekeeper is the mother of possibilities and adventure, the bringer of awe and arranger of the puzzle pieces from the healer.

The main strength of the gatekeeper is to allow or to flow. Practicing gratitude allows us to give life the permission to flow through us and to give us the confidence to know that we can steer our ship across every sea.

The goal of being aware is to face every situation as an adventure. We don't go into an adventure knowing exactly how every turn will end or what we may find; knowing that takes away the joy, the anticipation and thrill, yet in life we often do just that. Because we want to know what will happen, we do whatever we can to control the situation; life then becomes rigid and is no fun. Once this happens, we begin to complain or find ways to experience rigid-fun by seeking only those situations in which we know or are certain of the outcomes.

The gatekeeper is forever a child at heart, open to what life will offer and eager with anticipation to face each day with a brand new sense of excitement. The gatekeeper puts themselves in the path of truth and gratitude because they know that's where the light reaches.

They want to grow, so they are grateful to be planted beneath the dark spaces of the soil. They know it is necessary but also temporary and that someday they will reach the light. Because of this, they don't fear darkness either.

The gatekeeper knows that life is a cycle and so she/he keeps on with the flow, keeps on allowing, keeps on being courageous and stays open to receive.

> "Gratitude is the highest and purest demonstration of love."
>
> **–Bernice Angoh**

> "Feeling gratitude and not expressing it is like wrapping a present and not giving it."
>
> **–William Arthur Ward**

> "To speak gratitude is courteous and pleasant, to enact gratitude is generous and noble, but to live gratitude is to touch heaven."
>
> **–Johannes A. Geartner**

The Creator

When the rebel, the gatekeeper, the healer, and the creator collide, new worlds emerge. The creation of these new worlds is nothing but an outward mirroring of the inner world. The creator is much like the sun that gives and never asks back; like the tree that bears fruit for the eating pleasure of another; like the bee that makes honey even when its only reward is fire; like the rain that quenches and revives that which was once dry and dead. The creator is love. Not romantic love which is mostly concerned with self, but love that is spoken in action and is selfless.

> *"Gratitude is an outward expression of appreciation; appreciation is outwardly shown through kindness; kindness is an overflow of inner love."*
>
> **–Bernice Angoh**

Gratitude is an awareness of self in everyone you meet and a deeper awareness that all you have is most enjoyable only when shared. It is a pilgrimage between hearts where the universe is the only audience. Let me tell you a story that clearly illustrates an attitude of gratitude….

Diana was a single mom of five children who barely made enough to keep the roof over her head and food on the table but she never showed any signs of frustration or bitterness.

"But mother, we've barely got food to last a few days." The oldest said watching her mother divide the groceries in three parts. She had two best friends with whom she always shared her groceries. It didn't matter if she had one tomato, she'd slice it into three and made sure they each had a piece.

"Go, give each of them a bag. It should hold them for a few days too." Their mother would say.

The children could never understand why she insisted on doing that. They always thought they could reason with her but it was futile.

"What if we run out of food?"

"You will see, my daughter, the hand that opens to share is also open to receive. Have we ever gone without?" She'd ask.

"No, we haven't." they'd respond.

"Go and give these to my friends, they are hungry too, and they have children too. I cannot possibly be happy if they have nothing to eat. Whatever I have is theirs also."

Their mother was right. They never remembered a time they went without. It was like magic, that each time before food ran out, an uncle or far off relative passing through town would suddenly drop by with a trunk full of food; a bunch of plantains, rice, palm oil, eggs and some vegetables.

"You know, I just remembered you lived in the city and decided to pay you a visit to see how things are going for you. Come, I have some gifts in the back of the car. Children, help your mother unload the trunk."

And yes, even that too she divided into three, one portion her household and the other two portions for her two friends. But it was not only her closest friends she did this for, she was kind and giving to everyone who needed help; if she had she gave even when she had a little, she gave a little more.

"It is your mother you're talking about isn't it?" Lucas asked.

"Yes, they called her Lady D. She was mother to everyone."

"Tell me more, please." Lucas begged.

"An empty thank you does not fill the pot."

–African Proverb

"I remembered once when we were younger, I was eight years old and curious about why my mother always put food aside when she cooked. But it wasn't just food, she set aside toiletries and clothes. My step-dad had a good job at that time and our family was still intact. Anyway, one day I asked her to take me with her and she agreed. I was excited.

My heart broke when we reached our destination. It was impossible to think that, not too far from where we lived, in a beautiful five-bedroom house, our neighbor barely had a hut for a house. The zinc roof was almost completely rusted and rain dripped through the holes from the top. The walls of the cramped space were made out of mud.

In that little space was an old, worn mattress, a little fire side with three stones that held a little pot and a few plastic dishes stacked against the wall. In the corner, a little baby girl cried helplessly; obviously irritated by her cold for she had a runny nose.

I was in shock. I watched how the lady gently placed the baby down on the bare mattress and reached up to hug my mother very tightly. She called my mother 'maman', French for 'Mother', apparently my mother had been bringing her food almost every day. Her husband had abandoned her with the baby and having no education or skills to seek any form of employment, she had become severely depressed and shunned by her family.

My mother never made her feel like she was less of a person, she sat on the floor in that tiny space as comfortably as she could and played with that dirty baby as if she were hers.

As we were leaving, Mother promised to return with some cold medicine for the baby. We left without me finding my voice to breathe one word that day. That was the day I learned gratitude from my mother. I learned that gratitude was a giver, a giver who is aware of how much they've been given."

"You see Lucas, the word thanksgiving, is not just to speak words, nor was it to fill our bellies while counting our blessings. Thanks giving is the giving of self, to participate in the creation of ripples; ripples of love and kindness, the two most important fruits of gratitude."

"She was rebellious, she had walked through the gates and had embodied the healer and so she became the giver. I can't wait to meet her when I visit Cameroon with you." Lucas said.

"I can't wait either!"

The Seven Vices of Gratitude & How to Combat Them

1. **Complaining** sucks out all the joy in any given moment and where there's no joy, there's absolutely no room for gratitude. One sure way to catch yourself when you start complaining is to ask yourself two questions; can I change this right now and are there solutions to this? If you can't change anything at the moment, let it go, if you can, focus on the solutions, write it down and begin to see how to implement each one. Don't be afraid to solicit the help of close friends and/or family

2. **Worry.** Most worry is negative thinking. Worry is rigid-fun. And remember rigid-fun creates no space for possibilities, awe and adventure, it stagnates and suffocates. It's no wonder that in old English, the word 'worry' means 'to strangle' and in Middle English, the original meaning is to 'seize by the throat and tear'. Now, it's been said that 90% of the things we worry about never happen, why then do we allow ourselves to be tormented by these fears and negative thoughts? Is it because over the years we've conditioned our minds to always take this route or because it satisfies our need to be in control? The good news is that we can recondition our minds to start 'taking a different route' by choosing

to not identify ourselves with these thoughts. We allow them to 'walk right by' and consciously replace them with more agreeable ones. We must accept that life as we know it is riddled with uncertainties. Let the rebel in you attack these uncertainties with an air of possibility and impending adventure. This makes room for the healer to envision favorable outcomes rather than suffer the self with worry.

3. **Anxiety** and worry are very closely related. Worry begets nervousness and anxiety is just that; nervousness. To be anxious is to panic about over self-suffering thoughts about a particular situation. This is the source of all anguish. From the old French, the word 'Anguish' means, acute pain or 'tightness'. Some ways to ease anxiety and allow room to practice gratitude is to listen to music, meditate, yoga, exercise, eat a well-balanced meal and get enough sleep. If your anxiety becomes too overwhelming, seek medical help or other forms of therapy.

4. **"Un-forgiveness".** Forgiveness, like gratitude, is a giver; giving oneself the permission to let love take the place of guilt, shame, anger and resentment. Forgiveness is 'for giving' not to withhold but to extend a helping hand to oneself and/or to another. The one thing forgiveness does is to open the gate to endless possibilities. Forgiveness is the rebel handing over the keys of surrender to the gatekeeper and those keys are the keys to the healing room where all good fruits come from. Forgiveness is a surefire way to express self-love. Gratitude can never be expressed in an unforgiving heart; its fruits are most bitter to the one withholding forgiveness. If there is any guilt, shame, resentment or anger inside you, weed them out for they will choke the beautiful flowers

trying to grow within. An awakened person knows that un-forgiveness is just a slower form of suicide.

5. **Selfishness** is the mask of a narcissist. Narcissist never can truly practice gratitude because they are takers not givers. All contributions are made only for self-satisfaction and that is their highest goal. Selfishness prevents from seeing the needs of others because the self is insatiable. The room of love in a selfish person is empty. Gratitude is the purest and highest expression of love and what you don't have you can't give. One way to become more selfless is to cultivate the mindset of walking in others' shoes'. An awakened person often goes out of your way to assist and help others in need not for recognition or a reward but as a contribution to creation.

6. **Envy** is a self-loather. She says, "Because the other person has what I want or don't have, it means either I'm not worthy or not deserving and I'm not deserving because there's something not quite right with me." This discontentment with oneself fuels the need to possess what another has and resents then for having it. An awakened mind cannot be envious, instead it rejoices in the accomplishments and good qualities of others. There is an awareness, a shared joy in knowing that someone has gotten what they've open up for. An awakened person knows that envy is the laziest way to go after goals.

7. **Hate** is a synonym for fear. The opposite of love is not hate, it is fear and an awakened person is one who has learned to deal with fear. Where there is fear, love has run out of oxygen. Where there is love, there will you also find gratitude.

It is interesting to see that all seven vices of gratitude include either some form of control which leads to suffering and pain, the only cure for which is to surrender. Surrender is a mighty winged eagle.

"As the duality of life shows in every facet of life, as moon is to sun and night is to day, so too gratitude has her twin, her name is happiness, but gratitude came first."

–Bernice Angoh

"Gratitude can never be counted, measured or quantified; it is as immeasurable as tears, as infinite as love and as unspoken as silence yet as loud as the heat on a hot summer's day."

–Bernice Angoh

"The fruits of gratitude are only ever felt."

–Bernice Angoh

All who practice GRATITUDE are GREAT-FULL.

So, Lucas, now that you know all these, you see then that there is hardly ever a time to not be grateful; because in giving we are thank-full and in thankfulness we are open to receive. This is your time to go out there and create a world you'd like to live in and remember you can only do this by contributing through GRATEFULLNESS.

4
MARRIAGE

CREATING AN AWAKENED LEGENDARY RELATIONSHIP

Dave Elliot

Essential Secrets for Not Just Getting Engaged– But Staying Engaged in A Life-Long Partnership

It's a daunting task to be asked to write the definitive chapter on the art and science of not just creating–but also sustaining–an effective partnership that stands the test of time. Those two tasks are quite different. After all, any fool can fall in love. It takes an entirely different skill set to stay in love for the long term. In this chapter, I want to share how you transition from getting engaged to staying engaged over years and decades. How does one couple's love grow deeper over time while another couple simply grows apart? What exactly is that elusive formula that leads to the very essence of what I sought when I branded my company with the moniker A Legendary Love for Life?

In some ways, I wonder if there might be some sort of cosmic mistake that I am even asked to even take this task on–after all, my first marriage ended in divorce. That was humbling and not exactly a ringing endorsement of my qualification to write this. However, if I have any credential whatsoever that gives me the right to pen this chapter, it is that exact experience.

As painful as my divorce was, it was also that catalyst that lit a fire under me to dig deeper. I had to acknowledge that what I thought I knew wasn't good enough. Since I never wanted to experience that pain again, I sought out the best of the best in the field of human relationships to learn what they knew. Somewhere along the way, quite unexpectedly, what started as a way to heal my own very personal wounds turned into my own personal mission and my passion.

The new information I was learning, combined with my creativity and a desire to be the change I wanted to see in the world kept me on the path and wouldn't let me go. Every time I used what I was learning to help someone else, it literally lit me up with the desire to serve. I wanted to take what I was learning and constantly repackage it to make it better. I developed a passion for streamlining information and strategies in order to constantly make them more elegant, effective and efficient. My thought was that the better I could teach it, the more people could grasp it, learn it and live it. It was right about that time that I realized my mission was turning into a mostly healthy obsession. If I had to suffer to learn this stuff, I was going to make damn sure that something good came of it. It's my sincere hope that this chapter informs, inspires and empowers YOU to create your own ultimate love and passion for a lifetime.

The Key

If there's one single and deceptively simple element that makes all the difference in the world, it's this: Selection is everything.

One of the most common factors cited in any study of highly successful people is their choice of an exceptional partner who inspired and supported them through challenging times. So how does one discover that kind of partner and what traits do you look for in your search? In order to unpack that, let me share a quick distinction on human motivational psychology.

Human beings are a product of their environments, experiences and choices. They are a reflection of their beliefs, fears, hopes, dreams and insecurities. Perhaps even more importantly, they are defined by the meanings they attach to their experiences.

After all, it's not so much the event that shapes a person, it's the story they internalize about it. Whether it's an untimely death, a childhood trauma or winning a lottery, it's really not so much what happens to you. It's ultimately what you do with it that makes all the difference. So while it's critical to look to the past for clues about habitual patterns of thinking and behavior, it's also important to look ahead.

When choosing a life-long partner, remember that the person you are today is probably very different from who you were ten or twenty years ago, especially if you were just a child or very young at that time. Too often, we make a foolish assumption that who we are today is who we'll be tomorrow when experience and wisdom absolutely dictates otherwise. Divorce dockets are filled with plaintiffs and defendants who cite irreconcilable differences rooted in the fact that their partner "changed." However, when you consider that change is the only constant in all of life, it's beyond shocking how many otherwise smart people might not see that highly predictable shift coming. For that reason, it's critical to choose a person that possesses a similar "model of the world" to your own so that together you both can grow, morph and reinvent yourselves over time. Think of a person's model of the world as the structure based on their past references and preferences around which they make decisions for the future.

I know that's a lot to wrap your head around so let me simplify it for you. If you look, there is usually a pattern supported by multiple factors that indicates a trend. Based on people's processes, choices and the energy they create, it's fair to conclude that unless a radical change occurs, people are highly likely to continue to "reap what they sow." Put another way, happy people will find ways to feel happy. Disempowered people will attract circumstances that prove them right. Grateful people will find the gratitude and grace in even the most challenging of circumstances. Negative people will zero in on what's wrong every time. Judgmental people will find what's wrong and beat up others with their superior awareness so they can feel better about themselves. Compassionate people will find empathy for others and maybe even find themselves getting burned by being too forgiving. Just as in life, the key to all of it is balance. If you know your value while owning your mistakes, you can learn and grow while still taking measured risks. If you're kind and loving yet hold fair boundaries, you'll have much less drama and nonsense. If you're both positive AND realistic, you'll game plan effectively and won't take foolish risks again and again.

The key to long-term compatibility is finding a partner who possesses or cultivates a similar "model of the world" to yours. That happens when you both share somewhat complementary backgrounds, experiences, beliefs and expectations.

In my wife, Katrina, I found just such a partner. Even though we grew up on opposite sides of the planet with me in the United States and her in Australia, together we mapped out enough common ground to bridge the minor gaps. In getting to know one another, we discovered we both had similar histories, wounds, experiences and desires. We also both had a passion for personal development and a healthy amount of tools that were collected and mastered in order to support one of our collective highest values: we both are absolutely committed to building and maintaining what my company name promises: a Legendary Love For Life. It's that commitment, and our mostly similar and compatible world views, combined with the love, respect, and appreciation that we share for one another, that form our very solid foundation. Plus it's also reinforced by the fact that we both went through so much before we found one another so the combined gratitude makes us even stronger. So essentially, we both have a collective vision of what we want our life and love to look like...a relationship "North Star," if you will. With our feet firmly rooted in the present and one eye on what we want to create in the future, we can consciously evolve over time. Even if we drift off course for a short period of time, we can still correct and continue in the direction of what we want to create.

The Power of a Shared Vision

I don't really know of anyone who accomplished any worthy goal without ever first conceiving it in their mind. Clearly, creating a mutually fulfilling, exclusive relationship that stands the test of time qualifies as a worthy goal. If it was easy, everyone would do it and we know that is far from the case.

We also know from past experience that when one fails to have a vision, one is usually sucked into someone else's vision.

The magic is in finding your powerful why and answering the question, "for what noble purpose do I want this?" Just as a hint, a "noble" purpose would be one that serves not just you but others, or even society at large.

Obviously, there's nothing wrong with wanting an incredible relationship for your own reasons but any time you connect with an intention to serve others also, whether it's your partner, your children, your family, your peers or even the globe, a magic is unleashed that magnifies possibility. It also connects us to the kind of compelling future that serves as a guide to stay on track toward the goal you have set.

What does a shared vision look like?

Some time ago, I was invited on a TV program to discuss a celebrity's highly publicized and very quick divorce. Instead of pontificating on someone's private affairs, I used the situation as a teachable moment and created an acronym based on 7 critical areas to resolve if you want a deep and long-lasting relationship or marriage. I Call It The A.L.L.W.A.Y.S. Formula™ and it's an excellent checklist to assess whether your most important values are in alignment. I share it here because it's a simple overview that will quickly reveal any major disconnects. As you review my criteria, please note that you don't need to find a partner who's IDENTICAL. You simply need one who is complementary. Whether you're single and looking or been in a relationship for decades, these seven factors will either be the glue that binds you or they will be the painful bumps and bruises that could potentially tear you apart.

Aspirations & Dreams

It's important to determine what you both aspire to create in life. Where and how do you want to live? Are you an entrepreneur or do you prefer a steady paycheck and benefits? Jetsetter or homebody? It would be impossible to make one another's dreams come true, if your dreams are in conflict.

Links to Family

Do you have a workable family vision? Is your family close and ever- present or estranged and distant? How do you feel about caring for aged parents? Do you believe in an open door and welcome mat or a no trespassing sign? Family dynamics need to be considered if you want to make a great decision for your future.

Lifestyle/Health

Have both of you been up front about current health issues & long-term values related to health and wellness? What do you believe about exercise and diet? Are you a junk food junkie or a vegan gym junkie? Long distance runner or couch potato? Can you see how critical it is to make a healthy distinction in this area?

Wealth & Finance

Money issues are the number one stressor in relationships. Are you a scrimper and saver or a spendthrift with maxed-out credit? Are you an owe-r or an owner? Saving for retirement or worrying about that "later?" These are huge questions and it's so much smarter to see how it all adds up early than to pay dearly later.

Always Faithful

Do you have the same values & expectations around fidelity and monogamy? Can you be satisfied with just one partner for the rest of your life or does that sound like a life sentence without parole to you? Marriage or common law partner? Is cheating an absolute deal-breaker or are you okay with an open relationship? Where exactly do you draw the line?

Youth & Children

When it comes to children and families, do you believe "the bigger, the better" or have you decided kids aren't for you? Do you want them now or maybe later? Would you adopt or be willing to pay for in vitro fertilization if you had trouble conceiving? What do you believe about discipline? Public school vs private? This is a huge issue and like kids...it only gets bigger over time.

Spirituality/Religious Beliefs

How important is a spiritual life to you? Are you devoutly religious or atheist? What holiday traditions or rituals do you observe faithfully? Would you baptize your kids? How do you feel about religious schools, daily praying or regular worship? Oftentimes, spiritual beliefs will change and shift over time but they are deeply tied to your identity so it's important that you approach this area with mutual respect and appreciation.

The Last Word–A.L.L.W.A.Y.S.

As you can see, there are a number of really huge topics that need to be understood by both partners before you can successfully settle down and have what it takes to be together always. The bottom line is if you really want to have a storybook romance, it all comes down to both parties being on the same page.

Beyond Selection

Even though this chapter is all about creating an effective, long-lasting partnership, I have purposely focused half of it on finding the right partner. That should tell you just how important selection is in your ultimate success. Plus, I've even covered some key areas where you can re-build and realign with the partner you already have if that's where you are currently. Beyond that, I want to share the specific tool I use most often to repair relationships in trouble. The reason it's so effective is that it allows me to diagnose exactly what's missing from a relationship that once worked and it gives me a framework to teach the specific awareness and skill that can turn it all around for good. I'll get to the specifics of that tool shortly.

Once you've identified an excellent prospective lifetime partner and made the commitment to doing what it takes to create an incredibly healthy and fulfilling love, the next step is asking yourself three fundamental questions. In asking these questions, you begin to focus on the road ahead and exactly what you need to be successful for the long term.

Does this person deserve to be loved in exactly the way they need to be loved?

This is not meant to be a trick question, but sometimes, it can become one if you don't know and embody one simple distinction that can literally be the difference between success and failure in an intimate relationship.

Most people are familiar with The Golden Rule, a spiritual and biblical principle (Luke 6:31). There are several translations but the basic wording is "Do to Others as You Would Have Them Do to You." While that's a nice thought regarding the power of reciprocity, people who get married believing that may run into trouble. That's because there's a Platinum Rule that overrules it. While the wording is pretty similar, the effect is profoundly different because The Platinum Rule says "Treat Others the Way THEY NEED to Be Treated."

Can you see what a huge difference a subtle change in verbiage can make? Rather than "Treat Others the Way You Want to Be Treated," instead you "Treat Others the Way THEY NEED to Be Treated." That is a game changer! Simply taking the focus off of self and placing it on your partner changes everything. It also properly prioritizes giving over getting and that tends to unleash reciprocation and total gratitude in your partner. Imagine what's possible when two people are both doing their very best to fill up and delight their partner? I've never seen a relationship end when both partners are playing at that level. It just doesn't happen.

It can be absolutely revolutionary to realize that your partner needs to be treated in a certain way and that may be quite different from your own preference. I can tell you after a lot of experience working through couple's deepest, most painful disconnects, quite often, both frustrated partner's still love one another in their own way–and THAT is exactly the problem. They love the partner in the way they themselves want to be loved. This simple realization can lead to miracles and it also leads to my next question:

Do you want to be right or do you want to be in love?

A miracle is simply a change in perception that can change everything. When a relationship has some challenges, there are usually two primary responses.

The first is to deny and defy. That's when one or both partners throw accusations at the other and they communicate in complaints rather than in requests. They expect and look for disappointments so they find them easily and often. Then, since vindication is more important than appreciation, they not only attack their partner, they lobby for support from outsiders. It's public relations at its worst and it's incredibly damaging. In fact, sometimes my biggest challenge in repairing a relationship is breaking the addiction to this low-quality, habit-forming and corrosive payoff. An outsider's pity is a terrible substitute for true, unconditional love.

The better response is to be open and honest. It's about being a mature adult and asking "what was my role in that issue?" It's about resolving your old wounds and showing up whole and healed. It's about owning it when you fall short, committing to be better and letting go of righteousness. It's about gracefully accepting an apology and working to get back on track. It's giving up your need for vindication and letting go of your ego's focus on "me" in favor of the collective "we." Once I help my clients get here, miracles happen. I've seen them withdraw divorce papers. I've watched them go deeper than ever before, rebuild trust when it's been completely shattered and heal wounds they didn't know they had. Once we get to this stage, the final question is the game-changer that changes everything.

What exactly do I need to do to not just satisfy but delight my partner?

This is the first step in mastery because it steps outside of self and shifts to serving your partner. For some, it is a lifetime of work and many will never come close to achieving it. The goal here is to become a raving fan of your partner. It's about putting their needs ahead of your own with no guarantee of reciprocation–although the odds are definitely in your favor if you've chosen well. At this level, you start to know your partner better than they know themselves and develop the ability to see the greatness in them even in those moments when they themselves don't see it. That not only transforms your partnership; it extends beyond the two of you and into the world at large, inspiring others around you with what's possible. Playing at that level shows your kids how to create their own Legendary Love for Life and potentially effects a family and others around you for generations after you're gone.

Once you commit to playing at this level, you need a set of tools that will help you get on track and stay on track. Perhaps the most important and transformational skill set you will ever need is an understanding of love or attraction strategies. Some time ago, I created my very first product so I could help couples master this exact skill. Most people have no idea what a love strategy IS, but they know how it feels when it's not working and they have no idea how to fix it!

That's why I created the tool I call The *H.U.G. & K.I.S.S. Hierarchy*™. As you might suspect, HUG & KISS is an acronym and each letter represents a category or an idea. When I teach new or somewhat complex ideas, I like to create simple mnemonic devices which are designed to assist the memory in organizing, retaining and unpacking information. If you think about it, when it comes to understanding how to love your partner best, what's easier to remember than the words Hug and Kiss?

In the *HUG & KISS Hierarchy*, there are 7 letters which means there are 7 strategies or Languages of Love. Each different need is based on the individual's past references or preferences. So a love strategy based on a reference might be based on a magical fairy tale, a past experience that felt like love or even a scene from a romantic comedy. A love strategy based on a preference is simply an area where you are aware of some contrast between either what totally turned you on...or potentially turned you off.

Then it gets filed away for future reference and since it usually combines a stimulus AND an emotion, it fires quickly, is quite powerful and can last a lifetime. Now let's get into the seven love strategy categories:

The first strategy starts with H and that stands for Human Touch. It's all about that longing so many of us have for physical touch or a kinesthetic, hands-on connection with another human being. Whether it's a gentle touch, a firm grip, the touch of two lips or holding hands, for some people, there is no substitute for human touch and if they are not touched just right–they literally can't feel love. Can you imagine? Some of you know exactly what I mean. Others who may be turned off by touchy, feel-y stuff and don't want to be "smothered" might wonder what the big deal is but it means everything to the person who craves and NEEDS physical touch.

The next strategy starts with U and that stands for Unselfish Service. Like the other needs, this definition means very different things to different people. People who need and prefer this strategy know they're loved when you consider them with thoughtful acts of service or kind gestures. Maybe it's bringing them their morning coffee, or making sure their suits are cleaned and pressed just the way they like them. Maybe it's the way you pack their lunch, or for some, it's the way you remember to take out the trash or help with the dishes. For some, it doesn't even matter if the acts are entirely for THEM–maybe they feel wonderful and supported deeply if you read to the kids before bedtime and give them a chance to catch their breath at the end of the day. Like all of these love strategies, it's not so much WHAT the act is–it's how it makes your partner feel and if they can count on their partner loving them enough.

The next letter which just happens to complete the word HUG is G and that stands for Gifts & Presents. Have you ever noticed how some people go overboard with thoughtful and perfectly-chosen holiday gifts and beautiful wrapping while some can barely be bothered? How about travelers who go on a trip somewhere and return with armloads of gifts while others view that as ridiculous or an impractical waste of money? What if those two people are in a relationship? Can you see how critical it is that two partners' deepest values and needs are in alignment? It all comes down to personal values and what's most important to the individual is that they and their partner are aligned because for some, the right gift literally feels like love and no gift equals no love.

Next, the K in KISS stands for Kind Words & Validation. Some people absolutely love to hear what you think of them in the form of kind words of affirmation. They crave verbal reassurance and like to be thanked often.

They are in heaven when lavished with praise or understanding and disappointed or hurt when "unrecognized" verbally. Even if you don't offer specific words of praise per se, the simple act of validating someone can be amazingly powerful with long-term effects. Sometimes the act of simply understanding someone and withholding judgment is a powerful gift, especially for one who values kind words and affirmation.

Next, we have the letter I that stands for Important Priority. Someone who values this need highly must feel like they are your number one priority.

They crave attention, value certainty and need to know that their needs will be met because they come first. They may "test" occasionally and require more frequent communication or demonstrations of their partner's commitment. It's also possible they could be very sensitive to any perceived conflicts of interest. The beauty of this need is that if both partners value it highly, there's an excellent chance it will be returned at a very high level.

Now we're almost done. The 1st S stands for Special Moments or quality time. A special moments person is all about forging a deep connection that is nurtured and created in the experience of life. Special Moments people are about creating memorable events marked by deep emotional bonds.

For some that could be a romantic dinner for 2. Maybe for others it's a long drive with the top down. For some, maybe it's a walk in the woods or even a family gathering. Special moments people are driven by a desire to create experiences or what I like to call "magic moments."

Finishing out the word KISS, the last S stands for Soul Connection. Someone with this need near the top of their hierarchy will highly value intimacy or sensuality and sexuality. They crave a desire for the concept of Oneness and might be lit up by the idea of practically finishing one another's sentences because they are so aligned. These people tend to be very kinesthetic but they also create experiences using all their modalities or senses like deep, penetrating looks into a lover's eyes, a heightened sense of smell and taste, or a total sensory experience of oneness. When this is your primary love strategy, your goal is simply to have two souls become one, connected at the deepest levels.

So that's The H.U.G. & K.I.S.S. Hierarchy. Can you see how using this framework to understand your partner and what they need at a deeper level can absolutely transform a relationship? The next step is that you and your partner review the seven preferences and rank them from most to least important to identify your Hierarchy. Then you compare them and look for common ground or places where you're both similar. You don't have to have a mirror image to be well-matched. You simply need to complement one another or be close while having an appreciation for your partner and a real interest in loving them the way they need to be loved. After all, that's what they deserve–and you deserve the same in return.

So if I had to sum this whole chapter up in just a few words, there's a very simple message I hope you take away. Just remember to A.L.L.W.A.Y.S.

H.U.G. & K.I.S.S. Or you can simply H.U.G. & K.I.S.S. A.L.L.W.A.Y.S. Either way, that will help a great deal when it comes to crafting your own Legendary Love for Life.

5
NOTHING LASTS FOREVER

How the Awakened Mind Handles the End of a Relationship

Dr. Jim Rogers

Life is messy. It's not at all convenient because we're not simple, rational cyborg units that are only capable of acting. As human *beings* we have an emotional component to this beingness of ours, and this is what makes life messy.

Were it not for these emotions we would be so much more effective and efficient in the way we deal with life. For the most part, we spend a lot of time doing our best to either escape or inappropriately express our emotions, most of which are the result of our stored, negative emotional energy. Yet, to be effective in life, we must learn to deal with this energy that moves through us as it tries to find its way to our surface to be released.

If life is messy, then one of its messiest parts happens to be our interactions with others. Why? Well the main reason is that they involve two different individuals with their own stored emotional energies. While these two may feel that they share a similar sense of "reality," which is why they have chosen to interact in a special, heart-bonded manner with one another, much energy lies in wait deeply within each individual. During the course of their interaction, this buried energy will most certainly find its way to the surface as a result of being triggered by some seemingly random event. When this takes place, these two who initially confessed their "love" for one another often find themselves at odds, which will often result in one, the other, or both deciding to go their separate ways.

Yet another challenge of being human is that roughly 95% of our lives are controlled by the subconscious mind and its contents, a great deal of which became part of the subconscious mind by the time we reached the age of seven.

The problem presented to our relationships is that our world is paced much faster than the natural pace of our subconscious minds. Unlike the conscious mind, which can easily adapt at a split second, the subconscious mind is programmed either by constant repetition over time, an event with an emotional impact, or falling in love with someone or something. With this built-in limitation squarely in place, many emotionally charged situations appear to demand that we make a split second decision, when in reality, taking time is the only effective means at our disposal.

With a greater amount of suppressed (voluntary) and repressed (involuntary) emotional energy layered and caked in our psyches, more is required of us on a daily basis. However, instead of being able to perform at higher levels, we often either crash and burn, or find yet another way to either temporarily escape, or inappropriately express, the massive buildup of stored, negative emotional energy that constantly weighs us down.

As humans we tend to project this buildup of energy within us onto the world around us. If our energy is primarily one of fear, we project a vision of a fearful, judgmental, punitive world onto our surroundings. Likewise, if the energy held within is one of anger, then one tends to see a world that is ready to get even with them. However, if that stored, negative emotional energy has been cleared and instead replaced with an energy of Divine Love, one sees the world as a place of beauty and grace… one that is filled with the state of lovingness everywhere one looks.

However, with the presence of the frontal lobe, we humans have the ability to hide our true nature by saying things that we don't mean as we continue to either suppress or repress this negative energy even more. This mental sophistication is what allows someone to hide behind a social mask, being pleasing to others while allowing their true self to remain in the shadows. Thus, the alcoholic, the gambler, the sex addict, the frightened little boy or girl, and more, often do a reasonable job at hiding who they really are.

It's this element of clever mental sophistication provided by the prefrontal cortex, that keeps so many from realizing someone's authentic self until months, or sometimes even years later.

However, there are an ever-increasing number of people who are awakening to their beingness, and in doing so begin to experience the joy of their own existence. It is this slowly increasing number of individuals who are constantly growing in self-awareness, which brings with it a sense of inner responsibility to self and others, especially in one's close, personal, heart-bonded interactions that one chooses to establish.

With the above in mind, it most certainly begs the question as to what constitutes someone who is awakened and aware?

To begin, the awakened, aware individual understands, knows, or intuits that we are all spirit beings in human form who are here to evolve and grow. In this we do our best to reach out to help others who are working to accomplish a similar goal.

This person also takes responsibility for their life, refusing to take the position of the victim in any of their life's events or interactions. They also understand that the spoken word is powerful and that one's own spoken words are best limited to those that are used to heal, bless, or prosper.

As a result of this deeper awareness, one is attuned to the fact that the heart is the most sacred part of any individual and does one's best to respect one's own and guard that of the one who is their companion.

The awakened person also understands both that happiness is found within, and that they cannot "make anyone happy." That to truly love and accept another, one must first learn how to love and accept oneself… and has done so. Having mastered the arts of self-love and self-acceptance, this individual has become secure within one's own person.

One who is awakened is also aware that if they are willing to accept and enjoy the pleasure of entering into close emotional proximity with someone, then they must also be willing to accept and face the pain involved in changing this emotional proximity to one of an appropriate friendship distance, as nearly everyone experiences attachment to some degree or other. Remember what the Buddha said about attachments?

In spite of being awakened, a change in emotional proximity with someone (also known as a "breakup") has a strong possibility of triggering the release of some long-forgotten stored, negative emotional energy in one, the other, or both. Due to this fact, one often learns more about one's partner in this phase of your time together than in any other as the mask now falls off to expose the authentic self. Each individual will handle this change in emotional proximity in a different manner.

Some will take the change reasonably well while others will experience a devastating loss. Some will need to talk things through while others will need to let go and move on with an immediate clean break. Yet there are those who will never be willing or able to accept the truth as to why this change in emotional proximity was chosen. An aware individual also realizes that not all unions are meant to last a lifetime. Some last until the lesson has been learned, or the unknown purpose has been fulfilled. However each interaction contains a lesson we're meant to learn.

Why do we choose to end our more intimate interactions with someone we've invested ourselves with? The excuses are numerous. The reasons are few. Some of both are listed below, some of which will be realistic and mature in nature, while some are obviously not.

- This particular interaction has provided one with the necessary lesson that one needed to learn… or one or the other has chosen to not learn the lesson presented, and thus it will be presented again and again until it's taken to heart. (Either reason or excuse)

- This interaction has triggered pain within that one is unwilling to face, so rather than accepting responsibility, one blames their partner for these feelings and thus decides to let go and move on. (Excuse)

- One realizes that a mistake was made in assessing the character or compatibility of this person as a suitable partner to share oneself with. As a result, one understands that the kindest thing to do is let go as soon as possible and move on with one's life. (Reason)

- One chooses to believe in the 'perfection of partnership' as presented by the world at large and thus continues to look for 'the one' instead of 'becoming the one.' (Excuse)
- The revelation of a serious character flaw that the other is unwilling to address. (Reason)
- An unavoidable change in the flow of life. (growing apart, a change in one job or life state, i.e. military stationing that is intolerable, all of which could be either a reason or an excuse.)
- A change of heart and with that an unwillingness to participate any longer. (Excuse)
- An inability to work through any differences and/or accept them. (Both)

If you didn't begin your relationship with someone who is awakened, it will be more difficult to bring it to a loving end than if you'd entered into it with an awakened individual. An awakened, aware man will be honest and up front with a woman about his intentions from the beginning. With this, if someone is unable to bring to the table what they represented themselves as being able to do, then he can let go with some clarity.

Unlike the joy and ease that many relationships begin with, most relationships end in some sort of painful manner because two are suddenly undoing the connection that they've invested themselves in creating with one another over time.

It's with this pain in mind that most tend to avoid bringing the closeness experienced in their relationship to an end. However, the awakened, aware man will courageously face this and do so with the loving skill, tact, kindness, and consideration that the situation warrants.

The variables in such a situation are important to consider. First of all it's important to know if the level of consciousness of your soon to be former companion is one that's either below or within spiritual integrity.

What? What is this level of consciousness thing that you're talking about?

Allow me to explain. We all are quite like both a transmitter and a receiver. The thoughts we hold in mind radiate outward and the thoughts of others are received by us.

But there are also, for lack of a better analogy, these universal radio stations that 'broadcast' different consciousness energies (otherwise known as attractor fields) out into the universe. We each unknowingly choose which one we 'listen to,' as we remain unaware of the reality of our situation. This is why some are angry, some are fearful, some are courageous, and yet others are filled with joy and bliss. Each person unknowingly chooses which attractor field they will exist within.

The chances are strong, but not absolute, that the woman you are getting ready to let go of is tuned into either a station that is about fear, one of anger, or one of pride. All of these will ensure that she views herself as a victim. When you break up with a victim, you have your hands full because it will be all about her *and what you are doing to her*. She will not be willing to accept that things have run their course and that the two of you are best off calmly parting ways.

However, if she happens to be one who is tuned into a 'station' that is 'centered' in willingness, or another 'centered in' acceptance, or even one that is 'centered in' love, then she will also be awakened and aware. With this, she'll be understanding and accepting of this change in state between the two of you. If this is who she is, she may be sad and experience some regret, but she'll also see the wisdom of the decision and willingly let go.

Let's take a moment and examine how the same breakup is perceived by someone at different levels of consciousness, beginning from the lowest level and progressing through increasingly higher levels. We'll look at these from the perspective of a man, a woman, or from an impersonal point of view.

- **Shame** – How embarrassing… I just introduced her to all my friends and now she dumps me. I'm such a lousy boyfriend and even a worse lover. I'll never find a woman who will have me.
- **Guilt** – I had it coming. How stupid of me to not see that coming a mile away. I should have been a better boyfriend.
- **Apathy** – What's the use? Guys always break up with me. I won't bother asking why… who cares?
- **Grief** – Now my life is ruined. It will never be the same. She was the best girlfriend I ever had and I lost her. My life really sucks.
- **Fear** – Oh My God! He dumped me and I just know that he's going to tell everyone we know that I was a bitch to him. I wouldn't put it past him to try to beat me up. What am I going to do? He scares me.
- **Desire** – What an idiot! She thinks she can break up with me. By this time tomorrow she'll be begging me… no, paying me to take her back!
- **Anger** – That jerk! I can't believe he had to gall to break up with me. I'll show him who he broke up with. He's never getting his things back. I'll burn them all.
- **Pride** – How dare you break up with me? Just who do you think you are anyway? I'm the best lay you ever had and you know it!
- **Courage** – It's not what I wanted. I really loved her and believed we could make something more together, but I'll make it. I'll be stronger and better because of this experience.
- **Neutrality** – Breakups happen. Not everything works out. Of course I hurt, but I'll be okay.

- **Willingness** – I hope that she's okay. I know how hard a breakup can be and I'm sure that she's having a difficult time with it. I'm really sorry, but I know that we'll both move on and be even happier with another partner.
- **Acceptance** – It could have been a lot worse. We could have been married and going through this, but at least we figured it out before we went that far. I know she's upset. It's only natural. Feeling hurt during a breakup is something that can't really be helped.
- **Reason** – I know that this sounds cold, but let's be practical here. Although we loved one another, love on it's own isn't enough. It's best that we ended this now so that we don't get a lot further down the road and make it that much more difficult on ourselves to let go.
- **Love** – I know that she's upset and hopefully I can help her calm down a bit. I know that things happen in life. Just because we're breaking up doesn't take away from the fact that I love her. It just means that we're going our separate ways filled with love and are better people for having had the experience.
- **Peace** – How funny? I was beginning to feel the same way; that we needed to let go of one another and move on. I'm happy that he feels the same way. It shows me that I was with a good man and I know that we'll both find someone who is better suited to who we are. He's a good man, just not a good man for me. I'm blessed to have shared my life with him.

The consciousness level of **courage** is the beginning of spiritual integrity, below which people are most often victims or perpetrators who are only concerned with their own gain.

One of the most important things that an awakened individual is aware of is that if one has found their source of happiness to be within, and has also released a large amount of the stored, negative emotional energy from their subconscious, then one is relatively immune to experiencing the painful traumatic grief of a breakup.

When a man is considering a breakup, it's important for him to know where the woman with whom he intends to breakup lies within the levels of consciousness. If she is at a similar level of consciousness as he, and both are in spiritual integrity, the devoted, heart-bonded aspect of this relationship will draw to a relatively peaceful conclusion and both will continue on holding one another in high regard.

Unfortunately, these two may have both started their interaction as those who used one another, but one may have grown while the other one didn't. If this is the case, you will more than likely face some unavoidable difficulties.

The most difficult relationship to draw to a close is the one that exists between two who are both not in spiritual integrity, as this is often a relationship between a victim and a perpetrator. In such relationships, a victim unconsciously attracts the perpetrator. At times the victim will be compelled to grow so as to end the cycle of being attracted to any more perpetrators. This is part of one's spiritual evolution.

When a man lets a woman go, it's also important to know her well enough to know what she will need. Some will need to talk things through with you over a brief period of time, while someone else will need an immediate clean break.

When one has gained a new sense of self-awareness as the result of an awakening, how does one now view a relationship "ending" differently than before, or does one?

First of all, the awakened individual realizes that life is abundant and that if one relationship ends, the world is still intact. There are others in the world who are willing to risk their heart to be with you. Many view a partner as "the one" and in this lack mentality they place 'their all' in one person, overinvesting themselves without realizing how they endanger their own wellbeing when they do. It is this higher level of emotional attachment that is threatened as the result of a breakup.

As an awakened individual one does not "hold back" from the relationship, but simply realizes that life is a delicate balance. With the majority of one's previously unresolved emotional energy having been resolved, one is free to love without undue attachment.

Another important question to ask oneself as one moves from coupled to single status is, 'how am I defining myself now that this relationship has ended?'

An aware person has a deep knowing of being whole and complete. The only aspect of personal definition that need change is that one is no longer coupled, but single. As such they are free to entertain the advances of another or to explore friendships with someone at a deeper level.

Where and how does forgiveness play into all of this?

No matter how hard we try not to hurt someone in a breakup, emotions will be raw and hearts will be tender. If our intention was to make the breakup as painless as possible, and the other person still experienced a great deal of pain as a result of our letting go, then we get to take the time to not only forgive ourselves, but become one who is better at making a more appropriate relationship choice before the next one comes along.

If a breakup is difficult in nature, we get to forgive anyone who has bought into there being anyone 'good' or 'bad' in the situation.

What things can we do as we transition from coupled to single status?

One important thing to do is to establish a new routine; do different things than you did before. As soon as you possibly can, do your best to break contact as well because each time you re-establish contact, you open the wound once again and then your healing cycle begins all over again. Change up things in your life in a positive way as you give yourself time to heal. Listen to different music. Examine all the elements of your relationship, and once this is done, you can begin the process of moving on.

As we transition it's important for us to focus once again on our own value and worth… to realize that we are worthy of love, even if this relationship didn't work out. Journaling to process emotional energy is important. It's also crucial that we neither try to inappropriately escape or suppress any emotional energy that's coming to the surface.

How does self-esteem play into our self-awareness concept?

With becoming awakened, most individuals have a much stronger sense of self and the ability to reach out to ask for help when needed. For the most part, their self-esteem will remain relatively intact. The aspect of self-esteem (as defined in his book, The Six Pillars of Self Esteem) that may need some attention and repair is that of self-acceptance. Breakups can, and at times will, take their toll on an individual's ability to accept themselves, especially if they are the one who didn't want the breakup. Calling oneself into question is a typical response of the ego and the awakened individual will need to let go of that response, knowing from the "second agreement," that everything truly is impersonal.

What are self-esteem builders? The best approach to building self-esteem is by following the Six Pillars of Self Esteem as set forth by Nathaniel Branden in his book of the same title. Those pillars are: Living consciously, self-acceptance, self-responsibility, self-assertiveness, Living purposefully, Living with personal integrity.

How does age and experience change our approach to ending a relationship as we grow and mature?

In reality, I believe that age and experience change the way that we begin our relationships, for those who are awakened and aware, because we have learned how to become more selective as opposed to being picky. A selective person knows who they are, the areas of compatibility that are less important (as well as those which are more important) and is willing to consciously compromise some of these in exchange for the joy of companionship and sharing with another.

Age and experience influence breakups usually by cutting through the desire to hang on forever and let go if things aren't working. However, one also knows the value of doing one's best to work things out. Sacrifice is seen less as giving something up and more as an exchange of one set of circumstances for another.

What positive things can we do to handle heartache?

As Carl Jung said, "What we resist persists." The most important thing we can do is cease any efforts to resist that the breakup has taken place, as well as fully allowing the flow of any energy of hurt, pain, sadness, or any other negative energy related to the breakup.

How does turning this painful energy outward to help someone who is suffering ease the own pain our own difficult situation?

This is a well-known phenomenon in the Twelve-Step community. When one is willing to be of service to others by giving what they have learned to another, they in effect are giving to themselves. When we reach out to help another heal, we take the focus from ourselves and place it on someone else in genuine concern for another fellow human being in a painful experience.

As we reach out to another in an authentic manner, we further integrate the principles we wish to share with them. In doing so, we gain even greater insight into our own forgiveness and healing.

Summary Action Steps for Relationship Endings

✓ 1. Journal about this relationship including your feelings about this person, the lessons you've learned from this relationship, the lessons you've learned from this particular person, the characteristics that won you, the characteristics that you realize you somewhat half-heartedly accepted. Also ask yourself who were you in this relationship? Did you remain the same or did you allow yourself to change for the sake of the relationship? Journal about all of the above, and anything else that comes to mind concerning this past relationship, every day for the next 90 days.

✓ 2. Write down five self-esteem affirmations. Say them aloud to yourself in the mirror every day for 30 days. (Affirmations are always "I" statements, as in, "I am enough." "I choose healthy, loving partners because I am a healthy, loving partner." "I love and accept myself just for who I am.")

✓ 3. List three ways in which you can serve others. Choose one of those ways and enact it within the next week to ten days.

6
MINDSET AND MOTIVATION
Choose to Step into Your Greatness

Dr. Nic Lucas

Awakening / Self Awareness

Waking up is just the start of the journey. Imagine those who first saw TV, or who had their first experience of the internet. This was their moment of 'waking up', but now that they were awake, what next?

One of the most amazing truths of all time is that we only ever have 'the moment'. Our past is an unreliable memory, and our future is a hazy imagination. People who are asleep spend their time in the dreamland of the past and future. People who are awake exist in the moment.

The moment is like a bubble that bounces along through time and space. And yet along this journey, you can never be anywhere but inside that bubble. Much struggle, anxiety and depression is born of people who resist the moment, and who are forever trying to be where they are not.

Now that you are awake, there is a lot to learn and all of the knowledge and action that you take from now on will only ever be in the bubble–the moment. This is not a constraint, as it might seem to you initially. Instead, what you will discover is that time doesn't exist inside the moment. Everything just is.

Once this is not only recognized, but experienced and embraced, you can become the ultimate creator. For by understand that you are only ever in the moment, you can accept full responsibility for the now and full responsibility for what you would like to create. Your many imagined futures can be attained only through the actions you take now in the moment. And for this you must understand some key lessons about what is referred to as 'motivation', 'willpower' and 'self-control. And with that introduction, now let us begin.

Have you ever watched a master illusionist make a large object appear out of thin air? To our minds it looks real and yet we know there is a trick. We are unable to see the trick even though we're looking for it. We might think about that illusion for years and never know how it was done. We need the illusionist to reveal the trick, and only then do we understand how simple it is. The biggest tool the illusionist has is our minds.

I'd like to introduce you to a master illusionist. An illusionist so powerful that you don't even feel their presence. It took thousands of years for us to suspect that there is an illusionist operating in our lives and it's taken some of the smartest thinking and cutting edge technology to reveal the truth. The illusionist is us; it's you and me.

We walk around each day with thousands of thoughts. We think that we are thinking those thoughts. For the most part, we think that our thoughts are true and correct. This is the way our brains work. We would be completely dysfunctional if we thought that our thoughts were false. And yet, many of our thoughts are not accurate. I'll give you an easy example of how our brains create illusions for us.

When an object is rapidly moving toward you, your brain will overestimate the time at which you expect that object will hit you. Oh, it's only out by a few milliseconds, but those precious moments enable you get out of the way sooner rather than later. Your brain tricks you into thinking that you'll get hit earlier that you will actually get hit.

But you probably didn't know this? And even if you did–if I threw a sharp object at you–your illusionist would take over in the heat of the moment and move you out of the way by creating an illusion and changing your perception of time and space.

This one little fact is easy to understand and demonstrates your brains ability to create an illusion, and yet it really only becomes important when you understand that illusions are in every area of your life; the illusions apply to the things that are very dear and important to you.

And now that you have a glimpse of how your brain creates illusions for you, I'd like to share with you the most important illusion of all when it comes to doing anything important in your life.

It's about your motivation. You and I both know that your motivation underlies everything you've done, wish you'd done, or are dreaming you'll do in the future. Many people will say that a lack of motivation is the reason things aren't going well for them in life.

Perhaps you've thought the same thing? I'd like to suggest something to you that might seem a little strange at first, and so it's really important to take the time to let this sink in. But first, I'd like to tell you a story....

There is a doctor who is overweight and unfit and who sits on the lounge watching TV and eating junk food in his time off. This doctor knows better than anyone that he should do some exercise and start eating healthy food. He can hear his children playing outside and yearns to be out there playing with them. He judges himself very harshly and loathes his inaction. And yet despite knowing and feeling all of this, he is still more motivated to sit, watch TV, and eat junk food than he is motivated to exercise, eat healthy food and play with his kids.

Think about it this way. This doctor is highly motivated to sit and watch TV and eat junk food because he continues to do what he wants to do even though he has all the negative thoughts and feelings about doing it.

So, in this example, would you say that the doctor 'lacks motivation'? Is that the problem here? Or, would you agree that he must be a highly motivated individual? After all, he is a doctor, so he managed to complete many years of grueling study and training. He also feels horrible about his behavior and yet despite all this he still does what he wants–he still just invests his moment, sitting on the lounge.

From this story, I hope you can see that we do not lack motivation. Instead, you are motivated to do whatever it is that you are currently doing right now. This is very important to understand, because this is helping you see through the illusion–the illusion that you lack motivation. It changes your situation from needing to 'get motivation' to 'changing the direction of the motivation' that you already have.

Trying to 'get motivation' when you already have motivation is like looking for your glasses when you're already wearing them. It's a losing game as soon as you start to play it. Instead of asking "how can I get motivated?", the much more useful questions to ask are "how can I change the direction of my motivation" and "how can I use the motivation that I have to help me get what I want?"

This means you will need to be specific about what you want in the future. If you are not doing now what will lead you to what you want in the future, it is because you are motivated to do what you are doing now—in the present moment. This is essential to accept with full responsibility. There is no blame or judgment about this, only awareness and understanding.

Once you recognize that you are motivated to maintain your current situation instead of taking action toward your imagined future situation, you begin to realize the power you have in your life to decide. It is no longer about 'lacking motivation' but about understanding your decisions.

Let's go back to our story of the Doctor who loathes himself. Instead of giving up and thinking… "I'm just not motivated …", he can ask himself, "Why am I so motivated to sit, watch TV, eat junk food and not play with my kids?"

He can also ask, "why would I be motivated to exercise, eat healthy food and play with my kids". This is an exercise in mental contrasting. Asking these questions helps your brain shift the direction of existing motivation toward the future, whereas before there was no question to prompt this shift; only blame, judgment and an illusion that there is a lack of motivation.

This shift in motivational direction is the job of a specific part of your brain: the pre-frontal cortex (PFC). This is the part of your brain that imagines the future. It is very different from the thinking that goes on in your mid-brain.

Your mid-brain has little or no regard for the future at all. It is only concerned with the present moment and satisfying a present need. Therefore, to change your current behavior your PFC has to redirect your motivation into the future while also remaining very aware of your present moment.

The left PFC is associated with willpower. Willpower is required when you want to do something now for your future, that part of your present mind doesn't want to do. An example is exercise. The present mind is saying stay indoors where it's warm. The left PFC says this won't get what we imagine for our future and so we 'will' do it anyway.

The right PFC is associated with 'self-control'. Self-control is needed when you don't want to do something now that part of your present mind does want to do. An example is eating cake. Your present mind is saying eat the cake—it's an easy hit of energy. Your right PFC is saying this won't get you the future you want, so we won't have the cake.

There's an important practical tip for you to understand about your PFC. Willpower and self-control are very energy expensive on your brain. If you spend a lot of time in willpower or self-control you will find yourself exhausted and far more likely to lapse back into present moment decisions that are instantly gratifying and aren't influenced by the future. This is not because of a defect or weakness in you as person. It is the result of an under-trained PFC. The great news is that both willpower and self-control can be increased. You can strengthen this part of your brain with practice.

There's one more key part to the illusion that I need to explain, but before I do, let's go over what we've covered so far.

- Your mind is a master illusionist and most of the time these illusions are for your benefit
- You do not lack motivation, but instead you can learn to control the direction of your substantial motivation
- Thinking about the future happens in your Pre Frontal Cortex which is also where your willpower and self-control come from.

- Willpower and self-control are very energy expensive and when they get exhausted you are more likely to focus on immediate wants and needs
- Through practice you can increase the strength of your willpower and self-control and this will help you continue to focus on actions that create the future you imagine

The next part of the illusion to reveal comes as quite a shock to some people, although because you've already seen the through the illusion that you 'lack motivation' I'm confident you'll enjoy seeing behind this next trick. We're going to talk about 'mindset'.

When people talk to you about your mindset, they are over simplifying the way your brain works. The idea of a 'mindset' has been useful over the years, however to go further, to transform our thinking and our lives, we need better quality ideas. And we can draw on these ideas from research about how our brains work.

There isn't one 'mind' in your brain, and if you look at the term 'mind set' you can flip it around to realize that there are a 'set of minds'. We've suspected that this is how it works for a long time. Have you ever used the phrase "I'm in two minds about this…"? These minds of ours have uniquely different agendas for us, and when those agendas are conflicting we experience this as distress, angst, and indecision.

I'm going to introduce you to seven of your 'minds' and when you read through these, I want you to think about the decisions you think 'you' made in the past, and instead realize that it was one of your 'minds' that actually made those decisions. Here are the seven minds:

1. One mind is about protection.

2. One mind is about disease avoidance.

3. Another mind is about our social lives.

4. Another mind is just concerned with getting and maintaining status.

5. Another mind is only concerned with genetic replication.

6. Another mind is about protecting and supporting your family unit.

7. And we have another mind that is all about those in our community.

The 'protection' mind isn't concerned with your status, your family, your friends or anything other than protecting you from harm. It's not about reason, or logic or being polite or politically correct. It thinks and acts fast. It would rather be safe than sorry. It errs on the side of caution. In fact, I've already introduced you to your 'protection' mind, it's the one that creates the illusion that an object travelling toward you will hit you sooner than it will actually hit you. Can you remember a time when everything else has gone out of your mind except the immediate need for protection?

The 'disease avoidance' mind has only one agenda and that is to protect you from disease. Like the 'protection' mind, the disease avoidance mind is not concerned with being polite, or logical, or politically correct. It will strongly prompt you to avoid things and people that look different or smell different, and if it's food or liquid, taste different. When you're at the airport and you see people wearing facemasks to prevent them from catching a virus, this is their 'disease avoidance' mind making decisions.

The 'social' mind is only concerned with friendship, gaining acceptance within a group, and avoiding embarrassment or loss of friendship. This is a very important and influential mind and like the others, has nothing to do with logic. This mind will prompt you to act in whichever way will foster friendship and social acceptance.

This is the basis of the 'peer pressure' with which we are all so familiar and is also part of the reason Facebook and other social media apps are so successful.

The 'status' mind is very powerful and its effects can be felt resonating all around the world. It has only one objective and that is to get and maintain your status amongst the people you deem as important. The 'status' mind explains the extremes that people will go to avoid 'losing face'. If you've ever been in an argument in which you were more concerned about 'winning' than you were about the details of the argument, then that's your 'status' mind making decisions.

Negotiations don't go well when the status mind is running the show. When people don't like being 'wrong', that's the 'status' mind. When people feel enraged about an embarrassing situation, that's the 'status' mind. In fact, the very feeling of embarrassment is produced by the 'status' mind.

The status mind is also the cause of much violence, especially amongst male youths aged 18-24. When one youth is threatened by someone else's presence, size, popularity, possessions or wealth, it is his 'status' mind that is threatened and that decides to use violence to maintain his status and diminish the status of others. When arguments and fights break out over relationships, sport teams, political or religious ideas, often it's the 'status' mind calling the shots.

Some people spend their entire life in conflict, leaving a trail of damaged relationships and missing out on many wonderful opportunities that life has to offer, purely because their 'status' mind is making most of their decisions, overriding their 'social' mind and very often overriding their 'protection' mind.

The 'status' mind isn't 'good' or 'bad'. Like all of our 'minds', it's important to view as being a vital part of our human experience and existence. Status drives progress; it's what causes people to seek leadership; it's what gives people the courage to stand up for something different and go against the crowd. Without the 'status' mind we'd all be sheep, only motivated to maintain the status quo.

The 'genetic replication' mind is one I'm sure you're familiar with. It does have the one track mind label, but it's broader than just thinking about sex. It's also about attractiveness and romance and all the things in our society that lead up to, and are part of, genetic replication. Thinking of buying a gift for someone you're attracted to? That's the 'genetic replication' mind. Booking that candle lit dinner for two? That's the 'genetic replication' mind. Spending more than you planned to on clothes because the assistant was attractive? Again, that's the 'genetic replication' mind.

Often when people hear this, they react strongly and say that they do not have sex on their mind–and that's a key point. The sexual act is not on their conscious mind, but genetic replication is on their non-conscious mind, and this is very different. It has nothing to do with being unfaithful, or having lust, but everything to do with our strong internal drive to procreate. Many scientific studies demonstrate this.

For example, when men are playing blackjack and the dealer changes from being male to female, the size of the bets and the risks the players take predictably increases. When skateboarders are filming their tricks in a skate park and half way through their session, two attractive women start watching from the sideline, the skateboarders start taking more risks and have more accidents as a result; although they also tend to achieve much greater success as a result of all this extra risk taking behavior.

When women are shopping for clothes, they will tend to purchase clothing that is considered more sexual (tight, revealing, brightly colored) when they are ovulating. When asked why they bought this clothing, however, they do not answer "because I'm ovulating" or "because I'm thinking about procreation" or even "because I'm thinking about sex". And the fact is that it's likely that they are not be thinking about any of those things at all! Nevertheless, their 'genetic replication' mind is making subtle decisions for them behind the scenes that they don't consciously realize.

As another example, men give larger tips when they are primed to be in a romantic mood, whereas women talk more about the charities they support when they are primed to be romantic. And how are they primed? It's easy. All you have to do is talk about or show images of romance, relationships, or attractive people. Other ways researchers prime their participants is to have them write a one paragraph story about their first boyfriend or girlfriend, or about an ideal date. It doesn't take much to trigger the 'genetic replication' mind to start making the decisions.

Once you've actually met your mate, procreated, and genetically replicated your genes, you have a family–a spouse and children. This is when the 'family' mind kicks into gear and will make decisions focused specifically on protecting and supporting the family. That's why men and women make public vows, sign legal documents, and celebrate annual anniversaries. It's why they wear rings. It's why they keep photos of their family in their wallets, on their desks at work, and as their phone screen wallpaper.

Here's some more detail to help you see behind the scenes of your different minds. If a woman goes to a social gathering and is primed for 'romance' before she enters the group, she will notice and be more aware of the attractive men in the room. This does not mean she is the slightest bit interested in them or taking any action to pursue them, but she will notice them. On the other hand, if she is primed for 'family' before she enters the group, she will notice and be more aware of the attractive women in the room. This does not mean they are a threat to her or that she is even thinking about them in that way, but she will notice them. This is another subtle yet very important example of just how easy it is to literally change our minds, the things we notice, and the behavior that follows.

Lastly, there is the 'community' mind–a mind that is focused on the wellbeing of others now and in the future. This extends beyond the immediate family unit, and applies to the community at large. This is because we have a non-conscious drive to support the community we will live in, because we know that the community supports our family. We know that a peaceful, supportive and productive community now and in the future will be the best environment for our children and their children.

Now that you are familiar with each of these 'minds' of yours, you might understand certain of your decisions or behaviors with more clarity. In fact, you might understand them for the first time in your life. And while revealing these 'minds' is such an important part of your awakening, there is something even more important. You must learn to see how these minds can have conflicting agendas, because this can form the basis of so much heartache, conflict, and indecision in your life. Let's look at some examples that might have directed your motivation in the past.

Example 1: You might be so afraid of the water that you never learn to surf, even though all your friends are surfers. This means you will miss out on lots of great opportunities and experiences. In this case, the 'protection' mind overruling your 'social' mind and stopping you from doing things with friends.

You might have been driving a car and had an accident from driving too fast. And you were driving fast because your friends in the car were encouraging you to 'drive faster'. This would be your 'social' mind overruling your 'protection' mind. Lots of young drivers are killed in car accidents for this very reason.

You might really want to win a competition or promotion at work and to be recognized for the effort you have been putting in, however your best friend is also entering the competition and so you withdraw and miss out on the opportunities that would arise from that recognition. There could be a number of reasons for this. First, your 'social' mind could be overruling your 'status' mind, because you might prefer to protect your friendship. Many people, who do this throughout their life, feel like they are always putting other people first and can accumulate many regrets and bitterness as a result. You might justify this as being 'honorable' and 'gracious', however this is usually the way your 'status' mind enables you to 'save face'. It allows you to maintain 'status' in your own mind because of how 'honorable' and 'gracious' you are.

This is the basis of the most common regret of people who are facing death. They wish they'd lived a life of their own, instead of living according to what others wanted. People regret not taking more opportunities in life and so become bitter, even though it was their choice all along. Remember, we are doing what we are motivated to do. If someone chooses to let others take all the opportunities in life, then this is their choice and they then get what they desire. This should be celebrated, and yet often there is regret instead of celebration. This regret is a result of the conflict between two different minds.

Another example is the conflict that arises between the 'genetic replication' mind and the 'family' mind, as this is the basis of affairs and relationship breakdown. A man or woman, happy in their relationship and family, find themselves swept away by another person. They have an affair that is uncharacteristic because the 'genetic replication' mind won over the 'family' mind.

Another example of conflict is 'keeping up with the Joneses'. People put their finances at risk to acquire material possessions by taking on huge debt. This is a conflict between the 'status' and 'protection' minds.

There are many examples of this in life and you will not escape the conflicting agendas. Yet by waking up and becoming aware of these different 'minds' and how they steer the direction of your motivation, you can begin to understand yourself in the present moment. You can learn to pause and understand which mind is making the decisions, and why. You can ask yourself, if the current decision is in line with your long-term commitments.

Without this knowledge, you are pushed and pulled from one agenda to another without awareness. You make decisions you later regret and can't understand your behavior. You judge others harshly without understanding that they are also at the whim of whichever mind has taken control, and you are unable to explain their behavior and you are powerless to change it.

Instead, when you wake up and see this grand illusion, you become more empowered to choose which mind, and which decisions, are most conducive to creating the long-term goals and commitments you have made. The contrast is substantial. You become the executive director of your minds, rather than being the ignorant consumer of the decisions they make without your knowledge. This is waking up. This is what it means to develop awareness. And through doing this, you will transform yourself.

The great news is that awareness isn't like switching on a light. Awareness isn't on or off–it is ever growing. Waking up is just the beginning of a journey is which your awareness will continue to grow. There are many ways to increase your awareness and change your perspective, and you are advised to seek these out and peruse them with enthusiasm.

You can take a self-directed approach, such as reading and talking with friends. You can also take a guided approach, such as taking on a coach to help you breakthrough and speed up your journey. There are many people who have travelled this path before you and so you do not have to go it alone. You do not have to waste time trying to figure things out for yourself, when someone could simply show you in a moment.

You might feel like you have to do 'everything yourself', although this is the 'status' mind making sure that you can 'prove your independence'. Instead of investing your life to progress just some of the way along your journey on your own, you could get help and learn how to get to the front as soon as possible and invest your life pioneering new growth and leading the way.

So, I think we understand each other and you're ready to understand yourself at an even deeper level. What I'm about to do is open up the inside of your mind even more so that you can gain an even greater understanding of 'how it works'. The better you understand your own mind, the better you'll be able to access its power.

You might have heard the saying, 'So a man thinketh in his heart, so is he'. This age-old saying appears to be true and many people believe it. The problem is that it's not entirely true. Let's understand why.

First, we now know that your thoughts are in your mind, not in your heart. Also, your mind has many thousands of thoughts per day. Some of these thoughts are useless, others are horrible, others are beautiful, and others are creative. In fact, we have so many thoughts that we can't count them.

As you know now, these thoughts can be produced by any of the seven minds I introduced you to: protection, disease avoidance, social, status, genetic replication, family, and community. In addition to these, your mind is full of thoughts that other people have placed there. Consider how many advertisements you see per day and then consider all the advertisements you don't see, but that still make their way in to your mind.

Have you ever found yourself humming a tune, and you don't know why? Or perhaps for some reason you really want chocolate all of a sudden. Each of these 'motivational directions' can be triggered non-consciously when your brain picks up messages from your environment. So, given that you understand the above, do you agree that you are what you think? Or is there more to this than meets the eye.

An alternative is that you are not your thoughts. That your thoughts are phenomena that you can observe. That thoughts are the tools you can use to be present and creative in the moment. The quality of your thinking affects the quality of your life, just like the quality of coding effects the quality of software. Which brings us to a very important lesson about thinking and thoughts.

A thought is a pattern of neural activity involving many thousands of neurons. The more you have a certain thought, the more this thought will tend to occur. This happens, not just in your 'mind' but in your 'brain'. It happens both physiologically, and anatomically.

As you think a certain thought, this causes thousands of neurons to fire together in unison, like a shoal of fish all moving together in the water. Then, as you have the thought again, this neural pattern is reinforced, as if the same shoal of fish is practicing the same pattern of movement. The neurons in this 'pool' turn on specific genes that lead them to develop an affinity for each other. They are now a group, a community of neurons, and they all fire together with increasing precision and specificity.

Each time this group of neurons fire together, they produce the same thought. It becomes habitual. It becomes predictable. And anything that triggers that group of neurons to fire will therefore produce that thought.

Although our focus is on 'thoughts', this neural pattern within groups of neurons is how the brain produces many outputs. A golfer has a group of neurons that produce a golf swing. They have a group of neurons for the tee-off and the putt. A violinist has a group of neurons that fire to produce a consistent concerto. An Olympic lifter has a group of neurons that fire to produce the 'clean and jerk'.

When a group of neurons fire together to produce a specific outcome, this is called a 'neurotag'. Neurotags are the basis of habitual thinking, which is why it's so important for you to understand them.

For example, one very common neurotag is the thought that 'I'm not good enough'. This neurotag doesn't only produce a thought, it also produces a body sensation and an emotion. This neurotag has likely saved the person from the embarrassment, loss of status, or loss of friendship in the past, even though it also prevents the person from taking actions that would produce the positive future they imagine.

Let's use this 'not good enough' neurotag as an example of how these work, and let's think about someone who has this neurotag and is asked to give a keynote presentation.

When a person who has the 'I'm not good enough' neurotag imagines himself or herself as a keynote speaker, they will run into conflict with this neurotag. The output is 'you're not good enough' which triggers their 'status' mind to think "you're not good enough to speak in front of people! This is a risk!" This creates a dilemma. One mind wants to avoid 'embarrassment' or 'attention' whereas another mind wants to speak in front of people and have an impact.

This one example is representative of so many struggles that people have in life. And the struggle keeps happening over and over again whenever the 'I'm not good enough' neurotag is triggered and conflicts with other plans the person has. This neurotag is 'protective' but stops people from so many exciting, positive experiences.

You can learn to overcome these types of dilemmas through the use of willpower. This is the basis for the saying 'feel the fear and do it anyway'.

If you remember, it's the left pre frontal cortex that gives you willpower, and the more you practice, the better you get. Many people have become great speakers by forcing themselves to 'just do it'; however, many famous people still feel sick, and some even vomit, before they give their presentation or performance.

Wouldn't it be better if the fear were completely gone? Wouldn't it be better if they didn't have to vomit or feel nauseated before their presentation? Wouldn't it be better if they didn't feel 'not good enough'?

Thankfully, there are methods available that can produce this outcome, methods that can stop the neurotag from firing, or eliminate the neurotag altogether. Imagine if instead of needing to have the willpower to speak in front of people, you simply didn't have the 'I'm not good enough' neurotag at all? Speaking would become a breeze. It would be natural, easy, and comfortable. The audience would sense this and also feel at ease. It would be a better situation all around.

This example, the 'I'm not good enough' neurotag, is just one example of the many, many neurotags that are firing in your brain on a daily basis–on autopilot. They are having an impact on what you think, how you feel, and what you do–on autopilot. Only by becoming increasingly aware of these neurotags, can you begin to understand the impact they have on your life. Only by become increasingly aware of these neurotags can you decide which ones to keep and which ones to dissolve.

The skill of dissolving neurotags is a skill that you can learn under the guidance of a master. This is something you will have to seek out. It is something you will have to experience for yourself. This skill will elevate you from a place where you need solutions to a place in which there are no problems. It all starts here with a deeper understanding of how your mind works.

So let's go over what we've discovered in this chapter:

You are already motivated, so you can stop searching for 'motivation'. Instead, you need to understand what's driving the direction of your motivation, so that you can learn to point it in the direction you want to go.

You have a set of minds. These minds each have different agendas and can be triggered by the simplest of things. Whichever mind is in charge, will be the mind making decisions. By understanding these minds, and what triggers them, you can learn to recognize the automatic shift in command, and make a specific decision about which mind you should be listening to, based on your commitment to the present and future.

These minds of yours interface with neurotags. A neurotag is a group of neurons that when they fire together, produce a predictable outcome. These outcomes can be thoughts, movements, feelings and body sensations. Whenever a neurotag is triggered, the outcome is the same. This happens on autopilot, which is very useful. If the neurotag is preventing us from our goals in life, then they have lost their usefulness.

Negative or conflicting neurotags will create a situation in which you will have to use willpower or self-control to create the future you imagine.

Using willpower and self-control can be exhausting and so we need techniques to help integrate or neutralize the conflicting neurotags so that we no longer have to rely on willpower or self-control alone.

These techniques can be learned under the guidance of a master. It's up to you to find that master and learn these skills.

When there is alignment of present and future goals, and there is absence of conflicting neurotags, we will find it mentally effortless to do the things now that create the future we imagine.

Practical Skills to Use
Mental contrasting.

In order to increase your commitment to future goals, while at the same time being present in the moment, you can use a technique called 'mental contrasting'. To use this technique, first imagine what you want in the future and how good it will be. Then develop an awareness of your present moment. This will create a contrast in your mind, in which the anything in the present moment that would prevent you from creating that future, will be viewed as an 'obstacle' for you to overcome.

For example, if you wanted to finish writing a book by Monday, and it was Friday night, you would first think about finishing the book by Monday and how good it will feel to have finished the book. Expand on this and think about the other benefits you will likely gain from completing the book. Then think about your present moment and the fact that you have been invited to go out for dinner with friends. This dinner will be more likely viewed as an obstacle, instead of a desirable social event. In this case, you are more likely to decline the offer to socialize and instead start work on completing your book.

Research has shown that if you do it the other way around–if you focus on your Friday night invitation first–you'll be more likely to view it as a desirable social event and the book will seem like an obstacle. In this case, you're more likely to go out for dinner, and put the book off.

Also, if all you do is imagine the book being finished on Monday, then you are left living in an imaginary future in which the book is already done. And since it's already done in your imagination, there is no motivational direction in the present for you to actually finish it.

In summary, to use the 'mental contrasting' technique, first imagine the future, then become aware of the present, and then make your decision.

Train you PFC with IQ Power

The quality of your thinking determines the quality of your life. One way to increase the quality of your thinking is to train your pre-frontal cortex to come up with ideas that are worth changing for.

One way to do this is to use what is called 10 power. 10 power is when you times or divide something by 10. For example, let's just say that you are thinking about how to generate more revenue for your business. By using 10 power, you would ask 'how could I increase my revenue by 10 times!'. This question will cause your pre-frontal cortex to start searching for answers and imaging a future in which your revenue was increased by 10 times.

As another example, let's just say that you have far too many arguments and negative conversations with people. Using 10 power you would ask 'how can I have 10 times less arguments and negative conversations with people'? By asking this question, you would trigger your pre-frontal cortex to search for answers to this question.

The more you train your PFC with these types of questions, the better you will get at answering them. This is a direct path to using 10 power in your life and seeing significantly greater results.

Clearing Your Mind

Many people use conversations to solve problems. They talk with people and ask for advice. Very often, this can lead to lengthy and repetitive conversations in which no new ground is covered and no new ideas are revealed. Instead of using conversation to solve a problem, you can try eliminating the content from your mind and make space for new ideas to arise.

It is very simple to do this, especially if you have a guide the first few times. First, state your problem, for example, "I feel confused about XYZ". Then, your guide asks you to say 'tell me something about feeling confused about XYZ". Your guide then remains quiet while you say what's on your mind. The guide doesn't add anything. They don't editorialize your comments or reflect them back at you. They simply listen, and then thank you for sharing, and then again they ask you, "tell me something else about feeling confused about XYZ".

This process is repeated until you have nothing left to say about feeling confused. Very often, you will feel relieved and calm, and it is also common for you to find a solution within yourself for this problem. This process is very different and will clear your mind and pave the way for wonderful insights.

7
THE HEART OF PRODUCTIVITY
Effective and Efficient Decision-Making

Penny Zenker

We live in a microwave society where response times and expectations are measured in seconds. Life is busy and your attention is pulled in many directions. Our lives revolve around doing things fast such as fast food, convenience stores, online shopping, and express lanes. You have multiple competing priorities with demanding projects and work, market challenges in growing our businesses, family needs and your health and well-being to consider. There simply are not enough hours in the day to do everything that you and the people around you need to get done. And that results in increased levels of stress.

With that all said, most people think that managing their time will make them more productive and find some resemblance of balance. Yet when we focus on time, we create even more stress in our lives.

Time never was and never will be a measure of productivity.

Once you awaken and embrace the truth, that decision-making is at the heart of productivity, your life will become easier, more focused, and you can take back control. Productivity is a bi-product of the decisions you make and the speed at which you make them.

Here is a short story how this awakening happened for me.

I had just been landed a sweet position as the Chief Technology Officer at a direct marketing daughter company of GFK, one of the largest market research companies in the world. I was offered the job after an after an extremely rigorous interview process with the chairman of the board.

After creating, running my own Technology business for the last four years and then selling it off to a public company, I was so excited of the thought to get back to a larger company. I was already thinking how great it would be to have significant resources and support system of a large company to reach the corporate objectives. No more shoestring budget, 24-hour workdays, or limited staff. Or so I thought.

Before my official start, the Chairman called me to let me know that I needed to start earlier than discussed, and that he wanted me on a task force to re-organize and sell the company. My jaw dropped when he told me that I would then become CEO of the entire group holdings. I would be in charge of five group companies and 150 people across four different countries. This didn't sound like the easy ride I had been imagining.

This REALLY wasn't what I signed up for. I wasn't even sure that I was capable of doing that.

Before I even started, I was building the story in my head. I didn't have this experience. Why should they follow me? I can't even speak German very well and a majority of the staff speak German. My heart was pounding like it was going to come out of my chest and I was feeling incredibly anxious and overwhelmed, even before I started working there.

After the first day on the task force, I was anxious, afraid and frustrated. I went to see Peter, the Chairman. "I'm not sure I am the right person for this position." I told him. He sat there and said nothing. The silence unnerved me and I continued my verbal dump to him.

"I have never managed this many people directly or indirectly, let alone through a turnaround. I just came out of four years of working ungodly hours and this is not what I was looking for."

He continued to just look at me in silence completely relaxed. "I understand you feel a bit overwhelmed at the moment," he finally spoke. "I watched you closely during the hiring process. I saw how you approached the process, the decisions you made on what was important, and the way you conducted yourself through the interviews. You are the right person for this role. I hired you for your ability to make decisions, what you do with the rest of your time is up to you."

I was more than a little frustrated by this seemingly oversimplified statement.

But the more I thought about it, the more I realized that he was right. I was making it more complex than it needed to be. As the leader of this organization decision-making was the most important aspect of my role. It was and IS that simple.

Whether the focus is personal or professional, your true power is realized at the moment of decision. YOU decide what to eat, what to wear, to lie or tell the truth, to be grateful or resentful, to laugh or to cry, to be stressed or at peace, to blame or be accountable, to focus or be distracted, to hire or fire, plan or wing it, to innovate or copy. There is no doubt about it, that the decisions you make or don't make determine your results and ultimately direct your focus, level of engagement and success.

Why is decision-making key to our productivity?

Decisions help us avoids procrastination and mitigates perfectionism. It is ultimately the decisions you make that will get you in and keep you in your Productivity Zone.

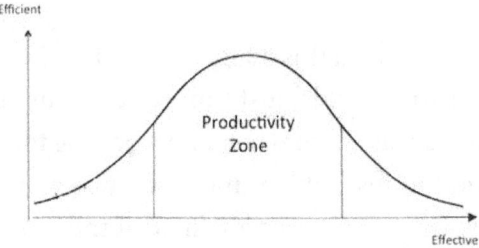

A fast decision may be efficient but not effective in results due to the speed by which it was made. The Productivity Zone is where efficient and effective meet.

Obstacles keep you from making your decisions

Before we look at how to improve your decision-making, it's important to address what holds you back. Is it fair to say that you often know what to do, but you don't do always do it? Awareness of those elements that hold you back allow you to remove the obstacles so you can either do what you know or get the lesson to create that knowledge and progress. Progress is Productivity.

7 | The Heart of Productivity

I use this approach because of another mentoring moment with my boss from above. From time to time, I would go into his office frustrated and demotivated, speak with him, and then leave feeling full of energy and direction to take on the world. One day in his office I asked him "How is it you always know just what to say to motivate me?" His answer was this: "It is not my job as a leader to motivate you. It is my job to remove the obstacles that kept you from your motivation."

What keeps you from effective and efficient decisions?

Stress is the number one productivity killer. It changes our physical state, which in turn distracts us from the tasks at hand. It takes are awareness away from the present moment.

Stress creates specific physical, mental and emotional responses. There is a physical change that happens in our bodies that causes us to breath more shallow. Our heart rate increases and cortisol is sent to your brain, putting you on high alert, ready to fight, flight or freeze. This has an impact on effective and efficient decision-making. As our emotional response increases, our ability to access logic and intellect decreases. That is why decision-making in emotional states can produce undesirable and unproductive results.

To simplify the picture, we are stressed when we are exhibiting any form of perfectionism or procrastination.

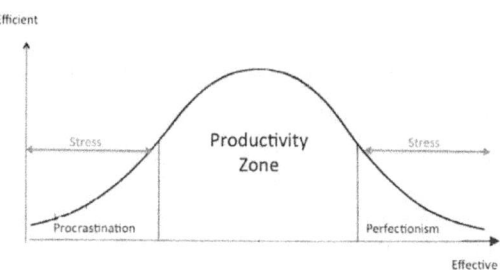

Pick your poison: Procrastination and Perfectionism

These are all signs and behavior of the evil sisters Procrastination and Perfectionism.

Procrastination	Perfectionism
Can't seem to get started	Can't seem to finish
Not the right time	Not quite right
No plan	Over plan
Not clear	Every detail
Denial	Blame
Ignore the decision	Doubt your decision
Excuses	Guilt
Frustration	Shame
Diversion	One more thing
Apathy	Critical
Scattered focus	Externally focused
Fear of imperfection, fear of success	Fear of failure
Lack of self confidence	Lack of self confidence
Unaware of Risk	Risk adverse
No expectations	Too many expectations, should dos
Boredom	Obsessed, Never satisfied

Recognize any of these in your own behaviors? Self-awareness is the first step to overcoming your obstacles.

Part of the solution is to identify counter-productive self-talk and in what contexts you find your self-procrastinating or caught in the trap of perfectionism.

Who, me?

I was late in delivering the business plan and all eyes were on me. How did this happen? I am not a procrastinator. I always start with the end in mind and plan my way backwards. I acknowledge my habit of over-functioning but procrastination isn't like me. I had to ask myself what was going on here. When I considered why I was not completing the business plan, I came to the conclusion that it was a fear of success. I realized that I was not 100% sure I really wanted the responsibility for this project.

The biggest driver of procrastination and perfectionism are often tied to fear; fear of failure AND fear of success. The two states often flip-flop from one to the other. Sometimes it is just too hard to be perfect and you get tired of never meeting these high standards so it is easier not to start at all. It is easier to put the decision or task off to the last minute so there is an excuse why perfection isn't possible.

How does that relate to your decision-making? At the root of both procrastination and perfectionism, decisions are not made in a timely manner if at all. You end up caught up in the unending loop of what if's, second-guessing, doubt and fear. Have you ever been so focused on what could go wrong, and what people will think of you if and when it does? You built the story so vividly in your mind of how awful it will feel with all eyes on you. You feel it with intensity and have all the physical manifestations of it really happening–it is your reality, but not the truth.

If you don't make the decision, then you can't be criticized or fail. If there is no decision, there is also no real commitment or accountability. You can avoid it all.

Or can you?

Breaking the pattern

A pattern of thought leads to a pattern of behavior. These dysfunctional or unproductive patterns of thinking hold you back from the very things you want. You are not unlike the frog that stays in the pot of warm water until he is slowly boiled. It feels comfortable and the situation meets short-term needs, despite the fact that it isn't good for you in the long run. Before you know it, you're cooked!

Break the pattern of the unproductive thoughts and self-talk that creates that loop of procrastination and perfectionism. Decide on the next step.

Decisions move you to action. Action overrides fear.

Here is my advice based on my vast experience on productive decision-making.

1. Get clear on the result you want

To make a decision you must know your desired outcome and connect to what will be different when you achieve this outcome. How important is the outcome on a scale from 1-10? WHY is it important? What value does it have for others? How important is the impact? What will make you do what it takes?

Clear purpose provides the passion and drive necessary to commit to a decision and see it through regardless of the obstacles. You need purpose to create accountability and follow-through.

When we decided to put a man on the moon, the United States Government brought in the best minds, invested time and money to make this a reality. There were failures, but they accepted and overcame them to achieve the desired goal.

You, too, can overcome obstacles that block your decision making by locking in the on the end result you want and need to achieve.

2. Get perspective

You can't find new ideas if you are part of the problem. The problem is all you see. However, it is only one

perspective. You don't even realize, the more you talk about the problem the bigger it gets. The narrower your perspective gets. The focus is the problem and not the problem solving.

To solve the problem, to find innovation, to create something new you have to step out of the current situation to actually see it for what it really is. The real problem is usually not what presents itself; it is often a symptom. When you get outside of the situation you can gain perspective, increase flexibility and solve the real problem faster.

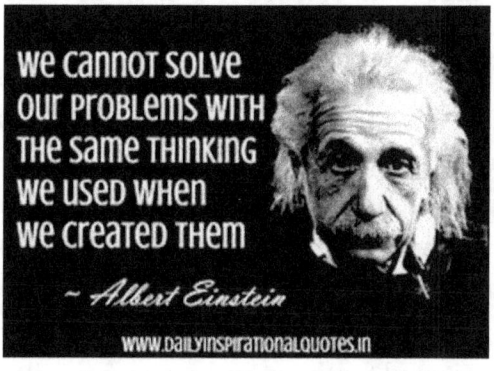

Efficient and effective decision-making is rational and lets you see things as they really are. Not better and not worse. Often because of the way you experience the event, your emotions involved have you see things better or worse than they really are. As I said earlier, when you are emotional our ability to think clearly goes down. Your brain literally goes into fight, flight or freeze. Then we no longer have access to our problem solving skills. This is not the best time to be making decisions.

Here are two of my favorite ways to get perspective.

Remove the emotion

To remove the emotion of a situation, step outside of yourselves and ask some clarifying questions of the initial thoughts you have about the situation. Byron Katie says to ask the following questions: Is this true?

Is it really true? Is it true without a shadow of a doubt? Steve Linder says to ask these questions: What does this mean? What else does this mean? The first meaning is usually charged with emotion and can get you in trouble as a result of your limiting perspective in that moment. These questions help you to get clarity on the situation as it really is. The more you ask them the more perspective you get. Then you can be the fly on the wall.

The most important decision we make and the most fundamental is determining what does an action or event mean to you. We make this decision unconsciously. By bringing this process into your consciousness, you are awakened into you power. You can decide, which meaning you want to give something.

These simple questions helped me manage my divorce in a way that I am proud of, helped me manage a seemingly incompetent supplier that missed an important client deadline, helped me negotiate some challenging business deals, it helped me when a client didn't get the results I wanted for them, and many more situations. People often tell me that I come across calm and confident. I think this is because I exercise my control by deciding on a productive meaning interactions and events in my life. The power of these questions has been an immeasurable gift to me.

How could this be useful to you?

Get a 360 View

Richard Branson is known for his risk taking. He told a young reporter that he doesn't see it as risk taking because he gets perspective. He asks himself two questions 1) what is the worst that can happen and 2) can he live with that if it happens?

How do you really determine what is the worst that can happen? Other scenarios? This framework aligns the heart and mind to support the decision through a combination of quality questions.

An NLP tool called Cartesian coordinates can help you with a few powerful questions set up in the following format.

Do it	
Would not Happen	Would Happen
Don't do it	
Would not Happen	Would Happen

Align the heart and mind

This framework has helped me with many decisions that were causing me stress and leading to indecision. After using this framework, the decision was clear and I could connect and own the decision knowing I have all perspectives on the scenario.

3. Define clear criteria for the decision

Productivity can come to a screeching halt if the team members don't buy into the decision being made. I can share from experience the great value of shared criteria buy-in: in one case, the implementation of a project that saved the company from bankruptcy.

While managing a technology project, we needed to produce top line data for retailers in a few days, which was a very different process than the in-depth detail it took us 20 days to produce. Most people were skeptical if it was at all possible. My team and I found a solution that was a cutting-edge technology. Many in the IT department were against our proposed solution because the technology was unknown to them. So they proposed other possible solutions within their preferred technology despite the fact that it was clearly not capable of the speed of data processing we needed.

Emotions and budgets ran high in this decision-making. It was the largest project budget ever requested. We needed to get the IT department and the management team on board. Internal politics and egos made the process even harder. Through a workshop with all involved, we defined the criteria together for proposal selection. With all in agreement on the criteria, solutions could be compared and evaluated more effectively. That helped place a focus on the problem and solution, as opposed to tangential and less significant elements.

Before you evaluate a new job, a change in business strategy, hire someone new, or even get a divorce you need to clearly define the criteria by which the decision is being made. This will increase the odds that you are collecting and reviewing the appropriate data when making a decision.

Open communication and joint development of the criteria makes sure all parties involved own the resulting criteria. People support what they create, so their involvement is critical to the decision.

7 | The Heart of Productivity

"In any moment of decision, the best thing you can do is the right thing, the next best thing is the wrong thing, and the worst thing you can do is nothing."

–Theodore Roosevelt

4. Own Your Decision

You will never have ALL of the information you need to make a decision. By then you are stuck in perfection and likely missed the opportunity by over-thinking it, someone else innovated the idea or just opportunity lost.

Malcom Gladwell's research on the habits of highly successful people found that most decisions made by highly successful people were made quickly with about 60% of the facts. They then focus on the implementation to achieve it. Decisions move you to action. Action with purpose creates implementation focus.

The fact is, not all decisions will produce the desired results. I realized that, to be truly productive, I needed to eliminate the blame, guilt and shame that I felt when a decision I made did not achieve the desired results. There are many reasons for the result but those feelings do nothing constructive or productive to help me learn the lesson and apply it going forward. I can have learned to let it go quickly so can you.

Stop saying that is the way I am and stop blaming your lack of results on someone else. Those actions prevent you from learning and prolong the undesired results. Indecision and lack of ownership push you out of the productivity zone, creating stress for you and those around you.

You are 100% responsible for your decisions, whatever the results may be. But also realize that the result of your decision or the level of your performance does not determine your self-worth; that is determined by your integrity and accountability.

> "Once you make a decision, the universe conspires to make it happen."
>
> –Ralph Waldo Emerson

5. Implementation: Just do it!

Once the decision is made, energy and focus can shift to the implementation. Achieving milestones and steps toward your goals creates momentum. Momentum is key in the implementation process so you can ride the wave. When I wrote my first book, I created the cover first to give me the anchor or symbol that the book was already on its way to being complete. It was the fuel for my momentum. With every step of progress, I made, the cover kept me focused. Even after the 50th edit. Had I not set the release date and told people publically and created a campaign, I might still be editing the book now. You have to find external ways to hold yourself accountable so there is no turning back. Admiral Cortes is said to have done this by having his men burn the boats. Success becomes the focus when there is no going back.

6. Adapt and adjust

Someone once said "No plan survives first contact with the enemy" conditions and circumstances change and you have to adapt and move quickly. Planning and contingencies are important but rational and quick decision-making during implementation is at the core of progress and ultimately your desired success. Decision-making doesn't stop when the big decision for direction is made; impactful decisions are made throughout the process. You need to be open to the various forms of feedback.

Back to the Heart

The human body is an amazing complex system. At the core of this system is the heart. It pumps 100,000 times a day and pumps blood through the circulatory system to every part of the body. Your decisions are the heart bringing energy to everything you do through action and direction.

Effective and efficient decision-making is a muscle that needs to be built and over time creates muscle memory and automatic state.

Lucas, stand in your power. Make your decisions wholehearted.

8
SELF-ACTUALIZATION

Your Spiritual Spunk

ShaJen Joy Aziz

Who Am I? The Start-Up of Me

It's time to self-actualize and go deeper into my being so I can reach my fullest, most meaningful creative potential. How do I do that when I am in so much pain all the time? How do I even find myself when I'm struggling to feed my children, and when I don't even have enough time to take a shower? How do I do that when…?

Humans are always changing. Our facial structure and our bodies transform over time, and so do our souls. Our learning and the way we perceive things, ideas, behaviors, and people are constantly shifting, changing and adapting. If we allow it, every experience we have is a learning one. Everything we take in gets processed and changes us on some level. New information has the potential to create new thoughts, patterns, and behaviors. However, it is the people who are able to adapt to change that create the strongest possibility of survival. Darwin teaches us that it is not the fittest of the species which survives; rather it is they who are most adaptable to change that thrive. So, to self-actualize is to be in the ever changing and transformational arena of this thing we call life.

The question "who am I?" is the foundation of my being. Without it, I wouldn't be here writing this. At twelve years old, I was broken in ways which seem unfathomable. I suffered years of sexual and physical abuse, and our home burned down with all of our belongings. Then, as if I wasn't yet qualified for mercy, weeks later my mom, Fonda Joy Segal, died in a car accident. The night before she passed she told me, "Dream of roses, honey, and I'll see you in the morning." Those were the last words she said to me.

The burnt home, the rape–and the beatings that went along with it–were suddenly nothing in comparison. At a time when I thought it couldn't get any worse, I got the phone call. How do I survive this heartache? How do I make it now without my mother? The remnants of our charred belongings became all I had left of what I knew to be solid and real in my life.

At the age of twelve, I began a new life's journey, having no idea who I was, except what felt like pain incarnate. I began journaling, and it was through this process that I discovered myself. Being able to go back and read what was on my mind allowed me space to examine and process a different me, one who had no choice but to express herself, because anything short of that would feel like death all over again. From tragedy to triumph, I discovered who I am through my life's greatest adversities. It is amazing how our adversities are the events and experiences which catapult us, and which help us to discover who we truly are, at levels previously unseen and unknown to ourselves.

When we have experiences outside of our "normal," these different stimuli generate new responses which mandate that we find a way to adapt, grow, and ultimately evolve. It is here in this process that we are able to see and use aspects of ourselves which were hidden before.

I learned the fragility of life and the impermanence of the sentient beings in my world much too young. Because of this adversity, it is my duty, my purpose to be grateful for all which is, all which is not, and all which is yet to be. Of course, I deeply miss my mother. The pain has faded and the sadness is far away, yet the desire to have her in my life is as strong today as the day she died. This heavy burden was eventually lifted from my heart because of radical self-acceptance. It was with this that I really began to live.

Vulnerability, which honesty necessitates, is what is needed to discover the depths of who we really are. Self-actualization for me begins when we authentically and unapologetically discover our true essence. What deep sufferings have transpired you and have made you who you are today? What helps you feel whole, present, at peace, and happy? That is your true essence.

Being open and receptive to your insight gives you the power to ignite clear intentions, because every choice and interaction you have has brought you to this moment. You see everything you desire is not "out there" somewhere, it is already within you. Of course, it's not always easy. Our society has oppressed us with stereotypes and societal norms, deciding what is considered normal. Finding a spiritual practice to connect with yourself and begin the journey of self-actualization is to have the courage to be exactly who you are, confidently and without guilt. From this authenticity, we naturally do no harm to ourselves nor others, and instead release ourselves from these bonds of normalcy.

The best way I know to begin a journey of self-discovery is to be radically authentic and vulnerable. Asking yourself powerful questions is an extremely fast way to get there. Self-acceptance and quality questions will quicken the journey. You already are your highest self, it's in there, in your being, and you have only to remember. Dig deep within yourself and ignite your courage to begin building your life around the answers you find.

Dr. Wayne Dyer sums it up beautifully in three powerful questions: Who am I serving? What am I creating? What am I afraid of?

Be truthful with yourself, dig deep and let the answers inspire you!

When you think you have found the depth you are searching for, ask the question "is there anything else I need to know?" Then listen. After years of teaching and counseling, and then training coaches and facilitators, I found myself asking these exact questions.

Purgatory

Jack Kornfield teaches us to lean into our pain as a practice to relinquish it. When leaning into my pain, I discovered purgatory. I'm not sure if I believed it existed until recently, but now I know without a shadow of doubt that it, along with heaven and hell, is buried within our minds. Finding the way out of the dark tunnel when we are lost and struggling to regain equilibrium is what I imagine it must feel like for a caterpillar becoming a butterfly: hanging upside-down in the dark, doing nothing but awaiting our evolution.

After a wonderful run of supreme success, I discovered that I had made some bad choices which ultimately impacted my ability to maintain life as I knew it. I was either going to become homeless in Los Angeles with a child, or I needed to make a drastic choice in an entirely new direction. It was this drastic choice, going back home to the snowy mountains of Vermont, which brought me to my knees and, ultimately and over time, to deep gratitude. I went from living comfortably in Southern California, sitting in the sun with a dear friend planning for our next group of trainings and getting excited about all the wonders that were unfolding, to focusing only on warmth, food, water, and shelter for myself and my child. Maslow's Hierarchy of Need really hit home for me in new ways.

I had to learn to cope with the emotional pain of living on the land where my house used to be. This land is the last place I lived with my mother; it was like ripping open the wound and hoping it wouldn't become infected again. This is where my work began, and amid the darkness of my deepest despair, I found myself again.

Rapidly plunged into my new mountain life and my immediate needs for raw survival, I found courage and strength I didn't know existed. Is that my highest creative potential? Probably not, but it sure showed me the grit I'm made of and the courage I have. That kind of knowing cannot be bought. From that jumping ground I started my healing. I am power and strength, and now when I'm coaching and teaching I have an even greater expanse of empathy and compassion that serves to help so many. I am profoundly grateful to have had the opportunity to get to know myself so deeply. I am the one I had been waiting for.

And that's where I was; leaning into the pain and honoring its origins in order to go through the grieving process with myself, and most importantly to be honest with myself. Strange as it may seem, it is my truth. I was a successful personal development coach, spiritual leader and an award winning peace activist. But I'm still human. Many of the aspects I embody and teach are about discovering the gifts in your adversities. I was about to put my own knowledge and teachings to test, so I took to reading my own self-help book in order to help myself.

There I sat facing my own words, my process which worked for thousands spanning the globe, and I honestly wondered if it would even work for me. Opening the book and reading my own words as if there were coming from a new teacher, I found myself engulfed in my story and eager to uncover more about myself and the next steps in life. Along with this eagerness was also the other side of what was authentically true for me; I was the saddest I could remember since my mother had passed. I knew it was time to do something about it when I realized the pity I was giving myself was only putting me deeper into the hole I was already struggling to see the light from.

One night while wallowing in my despair, and refraining from making a 3 am call to my best friend in San Francisco (because when you love someone, you let them sleep,) I began remembering my grandfather, Icek Lichtenstein. A handsomely tall, strong, and intelligent survivor of the Holocaust.

One freezing night, in the midst of a dreadful storm and frigid temperatures, he escaped by foot through the snow with his wife, my grandmother, Dora, on his back, and his infant son, my father, in his arms. He watched other men and families who had given up and were dying, or who were already frozen in the ground where they had decided they couldn't take another step.

Glancing at the dead bodies and frozen children that he couldn't save, he struggled with each step he took. He wanted to give up and die too. But something inside him just couldn't quit. With the weight of his world on his shoulders he kept trudging through the death that surrounding them. He looked down at my infant father, who was dying of pneumonia, and said "If you promise to make it through the night, I promise to keep going and not stop until we reach safety." That promise is why I am here today, writing this and sharing my story with you.

It is in our adversities that some of our greatest gifts are born and we find out who we really are. The power of my grandfather's promise propelled my belief in myself forward and my ability to dig deep within and pick myself up and keep stepping through the hard times. In the depth of my despair, who I truly am emerged.

Once I woke up to myself I realized that it is me, my own heart, that I had been searching for. That's when I felt a miracle; I realized the deeper my self-acceptance, was the more abundant I felt. I began to see the truth that everything changes when you begin to radiate who you truly are. The choices we make in life provide us with a window to who we truly are. Through deep self-acceptance and clear awareness of your thoughts and mind, inner peace is created within. Choosing to be in control on our own minds, as much as humanly possible, is where the power lies. Like the pre-flight safety check to remind us to put the oxygen mask on ourselves first before attempting to help anyone else, learning to love myself first was one of my hardest lessons.

How do you love yourself when you have lost touch of who you are? Getting keenly in touch with my inner knowing was crucial for my survival, and it was how I created positive life experiences moving forward. Remembering who I was and what I loved to do encouraged me to go back to school and complete a second master's degree in psychology. During this time, I began to have life-changing positive experiences which allowed me to be a beginner again; to discover myself in a new way, to reach beyond my comfort zone. This created a ripple effect within my family and community; larger than I ever could have imagined. After experiencing this self-imposed radical change, I deduced the pinnacles of self-conditioning to re-experience the positive and to use it to take a step forward, regardless if you've been knocked down.

Insight

You are not defined by how others see you. In fact, it is most important to pay attention to what you believe about yourself. It is in your beliefs that you have power. Paying strict attention to your insights and to the conversations you are having with yourself will support you in not losing sight of the basic truth. You are not your job, or the things you own. You are not a social media post or profile. You are quite simply living divinity.

Intention

Ernest Holms reminds us that where our mind goes, energy follows. Give energy to the things you love and always take energy away from the things you don't love. We don't have to wait to for circumstances to be dire or for them to be fully ripe to evolve. We just have to be willing and open to take action. The time to evolve is always in the essence of the moment. Seize the day and be clear where it is that you want to go and you will find a way to get there.

Integrity

Be honest and tell the truth faster. When I honor myself and my own knowing, and when I follow through on what I know to be true, the life I love living emerges. It emerges because I involve myself with the people, places, and events I wish to generate. There are many levels to integrity. Contextually, the most important level is the decisions you make when no one else is looking. What choices are you making? Do you walk by the garbage on the ground even though you see it and know it is your duty to throw it away? Integrity is multileveled and multifaceted. Be honorable with your word. It is the beginning, and often the thing most people feel the impact of, whether positive or negative.

Involvement

What you focus on expands. If you are ready to really notice how powerful our minds are, pay attention to what you focus on, and then notice the decisions you make based on where you have been focusing. The decision-making subconscious is paying attention to you and you're focus always. In order to make any change, you must focus on that which you really want to engage.

The key to writing is writing, the key to dancing is dancing, the key to authenticity is being authentic. There is a lot of discussion today about the notion of "what you think about comes about." Your brain's focus and involvement on anything will expand that thing in your world. Focus, then, on the political candidates you want to see in office and stop passionately debating about the ones you don't want. Try to see those you despise as very small children. Something made them hurt so much they began to hate. Release your own resentment and the authority or righteousness you have on it. This will expand your empathy and compassion and lead to greater peace in our world. Ignoring a terrorist won't make them go away, but focus your own powerful energy on sending your light and peace to them rather than expanding the hate.

Perspective

One of the reasons I love affirmations so much is that it helps to retrain the brain to focus on something positive. You can lean into your pain and concurrently give yourself positive messages such as "this too shall pass." Negativity has the neuro-chemical potential to be highly addictive, so when we spend quality time retraining our brain to focus on positive things, we will see and experience more positive events on a regular basis. We are much more powerful than we could imagine. When we shift our perspective, we change our world because we are seeing our lives through a diverse lens.

Perspective is such a beautiful present. I found I had no choice but to let go of a life I had spent 6 years creating. I suddenly found myself alone as a single mother on the edge of a snowy mountain. I had to let go of the life I had planned and thought I was supposed to be having.

I clearly understand through my own experience, the crux of the wonder of self-actualization. Using the gift of such adversity so that we have no choice but to change and find new and greater aspects of ourselves in order to survive gives a whole new insight to evolution. I understand it when someone says to me that they don't have the comfort and time to ponder such trivial and altruistic ideals. The privilege to find myself while I was quiet, safe, warm, and secure seemed to have been fleeting and momentary at best. I had to do a complete 360 in perspective, and my requirements for living did the same.

When your world is moving fast, as it does for all of us, remember to take the time to reacquaint yourself with gratitude and appreciation for the simple things and remember that where you are right now in life is not all of who you actually are. Self-actualization is a serious process, one which takes the sometimes painful work of getting in touch with who you really are, then radically accepting yourself so you can powerfully step into your best self and begin living a life which is active and focused on sharing your passions and gifts with those in your sphere and beyond.

Belief is a Power Tool

Being aware of our beliefs and how we really think is a large piece of how well we are able to nurture our seeds of intention in powerful and positive ways. It is action which generates possibilities. Inner action and interaction. Reconditioning our mind and emotions to unpeel the layers of onion to see one's self and connect with our most authentic self. Then the work is to stay honest to ourselves and to be congruent as you allow yourself to remove the mask society has placed on you and emerge into your fullness, into your authentic source of soul energy.

I firmly believe that the quality of the questions we ask determine the quality of the lives we live. My first question is: Who are you? Not, on the surface, rather, but who are you really?

Self-actualization is a process in both the conscious and unconscious levels of our being. It's reaching our full talent and creative potential that drives our needs and desires. The more in touch we are with our true positive passions and desires, the easier it is to create our lives from that space. Life is right now. We hear this all the time, and it is true. The work is to see your obstacles as your life courses, the lessons needed to support you on your next level of evolution. Focus on the belief of ease and simplicity of life and let life reflect that back to you.

Whatever you do, do not stand and face your fear. Instead, step through it and allow your positive inner wisdom to guide you. It is scary, but you are much braver than you realize. You see, when are willing to step through our fears, our vitality is restored and we begin to live again at a new level, willing and able to explore and discover who you really are.

You do this by asking, by seeking, by being open and receptive and willing. In order to honestly and authentically, and without editing, listen to our own inner knowing and take the steps needed can be the most difficult process. The separation between what the mind wants and the soul knows can be a vast gutter if the work of "who am I" has yet to be done.

Authentic Congruency

You develop your intuition by listening to yourself. If money wasn't a concern or need, what would you do with your time? Find whatever small ways you can to honor that answer. For me, I get lit up about creating a conscious and compassionate world. One where children get to thrive because the adults in their sphere have begun their own personal work of self-actualization and are able to extend their hearts to allow their children, who are often already expressing fully realized potential, the safety and space to express it without the harsh limits that conditioned us in the first place.

"Ask and you will receive." If you started being who you really are today–what would be different about you? How would your life change? Listen closely to your positive inner wisdom, allowing it to guide you naturally. Do not force any ideas. Allow yourself, even if it's just for moments at a time, to let all of your obstacles and history go and allow any negative thinking to dissipate.

Then listen–deeply. Trust your inner source. Hear yourself and see what emerges. To manifest from this space, it is crucial to take immediate action on your insight. Even small actions have a profound impact. Having integrity with your intention will create powerful results. Hop on and surf this wave of inspiration by taking one action today. This will bring you closer to your dreams and keep the fire burning. You are the one you have been waiting for.

9
HAPPINESS FORMULA
Journey of a Life Well-Lived

Gary King

Happiness is the most sought after emotion in the world. Yes, happiness is an emotion, not a person, place, or thing. Although by the nature of the pursuit, you would think it was external. Most are conditioned to believe it is our right to be happy no matter what it takes to attain it. That could mean it is a lifelong quest.

Based on happiness being an emotion, do we choose our emotions or do our emotions choose us?

We are led to believe from an early age that certain situations make us feel certain emotions. Is it possible that is behavior reinforcement based on cultural conditioning? Can we choose any emotion we would like to feel and not base it on outside conditions? Since we have little control over external situations, can we be taught to have enormous control over internal emotions?

We must first have a foundation to base our emotions on that has its core beliefs in virtues, values, and self-worth. All human life hinges on the depth of self-worth developed internally, and then the healthy self-worth creates our external reality.

We tend to suffer because we were not taught to realize we can choose any emotion when we simply disconnect from the outside source.

We currently live in a time when it is almost impossible to feel happiness and joy without some form of outside short term gratification, such as winning a mission impossible, finding our soul mate after a long search, or buying something new.

To locate the passion connected to internal happiness, we must start by not doing things that make us Unhappy.

Consider what you have been taught about your emotions. Is it safe to feel? Is it safe to share your feelings? Or will you be punished, rejected, or worse? Has political correctness taken over our reality and reshaped it into an auto-response?

Do we spend too much time over thinking our reality, rather than designing it the way it feels good? Looking inside and asking, why do I feel the way I feel? Did someone do something to me? Did I do something to myself?

Do we constantly live in fear and anxiety or in unconditional love and courage driven by the eternal gift of life? Do we dwell on what we do not have? Do we celebrate the air we breathe and the food we eat?

Have we lost touch with creating a happy reality and simply fallen into patterned behavior without even realizing it?

Imagine living a life of true happiness.

Do you even know what means to be happy? What it means to have inner peace?

I have read more than 2,200 books on personal development and Psychology. I spent 25 years in the personal development industry worldwide with the most well-known personal development speaker in the world. This gave me the opportunity to be in the proximity of six million people of all ages, genders and from many different cultures. I also had the opportunity to interview thousands of people. In their quest for happiness, these people paid a substantial amount of money to attend personal development events. When asked why, the number one answer was "to change my life." My next question was "what do you want to change your life into?" These were simple, thought-provoking questions for participants who were emotionally and financially committed to multiday programs. They would think for a minute and would respond with "I want to be more successful." My next question asked them to define success. Almost every person referred to financial success. Over that 25-year period of time, only two individuals said they wanted to be happy. They happened to be teenagers.

> *"Don't aim at success. The more you aim at it and make it a target, the more you are going to miss it. For success, like happiness, cannot be pursued; it must ensue, and it only does so as the unintended side-effect of one's personal dedication to a cause greater than oneself or as the by-product of one's surrender to a person other than oneself.*

Happiness must happen, and the same holds for success; you have to let it happen by not caring about it. I want you to listen to what your conscience commands you to do and go on to carry it out to the best of your knowledge. Then you will live to see that in the long run–in the long run, I saw! –success will follow you precisely because you had forgotten to think of it."

–From Viktor Frankl's
Man's Search for Meaning

Almost all humans are conditioned to believe that happiness has its source outside of them. In the history of human life, happiness is the most pursued emotion. In many western cultures, it's considered the pursuit of happiness. In some cultures, it's called the art of happiness.

I was interested in solving the riddle of happiness. What is it? Where does it come from? How do you develop it?

Even in ancient history, the most profound thinkers knew that happiness has absolutely nothing to do with anything external.

In some cultures, the world happiness is a derivative of the word luck. Happiness in some cultures is a product of happenstance. If something unplanned happened and it made you feel good, then you were lucky, which equaled happiness.

Happiness had always been an enigma. It had always been something that you chased after, and if you caught it, then happiness happened.

The challenge is most people equate happiness based on short term gratification and has nothing whatsoever to do with a life well lived. It just has to do with moments of short term gratification, which in many cases are developed by behavior that's emotionally unhealthy. It begins with childhood, and is based on your surroundings, your worldview. Whatever your parents and your immediate external world is doing and thinking, that's how you develop your worldview.

A child may have the perception that a new bicycle will bring sustainable happiness. That is not accurate because the acquisition of a bicycle and the emotion that it brings can last anywhere from a day to a week before the emotion wears off. Almost all westernized cultures promote short term gratification.

I discovered that 99% of the people I interviewed were managing the effects of their life. Very few people were managing the cause of their life. That's a universal law, the law of the planet we live on, the law of cause and effect.

They were working against the law that creates serendipity, luck, good fortune or any of the things that happen to you as a result of happenstance. Most people are managing the effects of the original cause. The original cause is found in childhood, low self-worth. We grow up validating our low self-worth, seeking to prove that we are unworthy. That is managing the effect, not the cause.

Think about life in tiers. The first tier of a human life is a physical level: food, shelter, and clothing. The next tier up one notch is to the emotional level of a person's life. In order to have a sustainable happiness you must have an emotionally healthy, emotionally balanced life. It does not mean that you will not experience pain and suffering.

Many of my presentations are based on the internal factors of life, not the external factors. I use my own life as an example. In my lifetime, I have had amazing accomplishments. I have also had the most unthinkable tragedies that no human should ever have to experience. To experience suffering and pain is part of the human life. To try and eliminate that from your life will make your life extremely unhealthy. Most people do not have a healthy emotional foundation. They develop the food, shelter and clothing aspect but, they live in an emotional world of deprivation.

Some of that comes as a result of the way we're brought up. It's the result of our westernized education that in general does not recognize anything other than academic brain washing, academic memorization and academic testing. There is no actual emotional factor in education. In addition, 67% of all the children were born to a single parent in the mid-2000s, and depending on what ethnic group you choose, the percentages go from 50 to 73%. That means that within that child there is a missing part. It isn't the fault of the child, but the missing part is directly connected to an ultimate source of happiness.

Everything in life has a formula. The water you drink, the air you breathe, the car you drive, everything has a formula. Chocolate chip cookies have a formula and if you don't follow the formula, you'll get something less than a chocolate chip cookie. If a human being is going to have a well-balanced, well lived life which also happens to be directly connected to the human immune system, then the second tier of the human life is going to have to have a really solid foundation which again goes back to the great thinkers of all times. They were clear that leading a well lived life is directly connected to a virtuous life. It is not connected to good fortune, because good fortune is random. If you check the statistics on the Florida lottery, the state I live in, you'll find out that the majority of people that have won the lottery realized that it did not enhance the quality of their life. It took away from the quality of their life and made it more confusing. Winning may have increased their material worth, while creating emotional imbalance.

> *The happiness of your life depends upon the quality of your thoughts: therefore, guard accordingly, and take care that you entertain no notions unsuitable to virtue and reasonable nature.*
>
> **–Marcus Aurelius**

I developed a formula that is very specific. It is so specific that it got measurable results in a very short time period, and those measurable results are sustainable. It isn't short term gratification. It is lifelong gratification. I know exactly what these three things are, and I've proved it over and over again. I've proved it through interventions, interviews, and through my own presentations worldwide with teenagers and adults in every imaginable set of circumstances: From speaking in maximum-security prisons, to third world countries, to entrepreneurs, to colleges and to teachers. I have a tremendous amount of empathy for children in the school systems because they are not being emotionally fed. I have a tremendous amount of empathy for active duty and returning military veterans because I was in the military. I understand. They are not given the emotional tools to create a balance that is in keeping with their level of responsibility.

I wanted to make the message universal and duplicable so that others can deliver the message. In order for it to be memorable, it needs to be thought provoking. I put the formula in the format of the periodic table so it looks like a formula. I came up with a sequence that I call The Happiness Formula™. The sequence is:

$$F2HT2SW=HF10$$

The explanation of the power of 10 is we have universal laws that affect every human. No one has immunity to universal laws. Two of the most powerful universal laws are the laws of cause and effect, and the law of compounding.

Everything in life compounds. Money compounds. I use the example in my presentations. I offer them $50,000 in cash right now or a penny doubled for 30 days. Most people choose the $50,000. Some people say the penny, although they don't know the dollar amount. ($5,368,712 is basically what a penny doubled is.) That's based on the law of compounding as it applies to money. The law of compounding applies to everything. The law of compounding applies to human emotions and human behavior, and it is directly connected. There's no immunity. The HF10 simply means happiness and fulfillment to the power of 10. Once you start practicing the formula, it's bound and controlled by the law of compounding. If you practice one element of the three elements it will compound rapidly.

If you research the penny doubled example, you will find that the most profound compounding effect that takes it from 2-cents, 4-cents, 8-cents to $5M happens in the last five days. I applied that same law to The Happiness Formula. The farther you go forward, the more it exponentially increases.

The formula is very simple. It's based on what the great thinkers and great philosophers have always known. The F in the formula is forgiveness. The 2 simply means there are two parts. You must forgive yourself and you must forgive other people.

Consider this for a minute. How in the world can a person be happy and fulfilled simultaneous to having resentment toward themselves or another person?

It doesn't take a psychologist or a social scientist to make a determination that you can't be happy and fulfilled while simultaneously living in a space of hatred and resentment. It's not possible. I would present the following statement to audiences worldwide, both to adults and teens. The statement is: "Raise your hand if you have no one to forgive including yourself. If you have zero forgiveness issues raise your hand." I began presenting that question 12 years ago, and to date 25 people have raised their hand worldwide. 25 people out of thousands. You cannot be happy and fulfilled living a balanced life, if you have forgiveness issues.

In conducting interventions, I would ask, "why do you resent or dislike or hate this person?", and they would give me this long story about how I don't understand what they did to them. The essence of forgiveness is not what somebody did to you. It's what you're doing to yourself. Forgiveness doesn't have to do with another human being. Forgiveness is a gift. You don't give it to someone else. It's a gift you bestow on yourself.

This research was profound for me. Sadly, 99% of the audiences worldwide had no idea how to forgive themselves and other people. They didn't even know where to start. Embrace The 24 Hour Forgiveness Challenge™. It will bring you peace.

The second part of the equation is HT2 and stands for honesty and truth. Do not get in denial here. Don't play head games with yourself. You must be honest with yourself and you must be truthful with other people without exception.

The way the human brain works is rather simple. The human brain automatically searches millions of files looking for a justification for why it's impossible to be honest all the time. That's what the brain does.

I've experimented with these many times. I did corporate presentations and met with CEOs. I've been told the most interesting imaginative stories. There's a term called cognitive dissonance. There's always a justification for a lie. There's always a justification for bad behavior, unethical behavior and cruel behavior.

There is no such thing as an inconsequential lie.

–Gary King

I am well versed in that subject of truth and honesty and why people lie to begin with. Where does it all start? It starts when you're a child. You were conditioned that when your parent asked you a question, admitting fault often led to punishment. The human brain then linked pain to honesty.

When a child learns that being honest causes pain, a survival strategy is developed. The survival strategy is to escape the short term pain by lying. Lying is subject to the law of compounding. So in the moment, they are escaping the pain, but in the long term the pain will compound because they will continue to lie and the lies will get bigger. In the 21st century, we have culturally and socially normalized lying. It's normal behavior. Everybody is doing it. It's a survival mechanism.

Stop!

You can call it a survival mechanism, but it is a self-destructive behavior pattern. Lying and happiness do not go together. They are incongruent. Lying causes guilt at any level. A white lie causes guilt, because human beings are born with what is called a conscience.

Many people treat their conscience as if there was an on/off switch. In order to operate they turn their conscience switch off and they start moving forward. Why? Because they've been conditioned that this happiness thing is a result of materialism or Ms. Right, Mr. Right, cars, money, yachts or airplanes.

They flip off the conscience switch and they move forward with the pursuit of happiness. You don't need a degree in psychology to come to this conclusion. This is common sense. That's why the great thinkers of all time determined that you can never have a life well lived if you have no foundation of virtues and morals. All you'll do is become extremely self-destructive.

Take The 24 Hour Truth Challenge™. It's simple: Be totally honest with yourself and others for 24 hours. It will change your life.

The next part of the equation is the SW. The SW is the root of the ability to forgive and the root of the ability to be honest. The SW stands for Self-Worth. I back engineered my own life. Assisted by a trained therapist, I went back to when I was a child, and relived my whole life and my original cause. My original cause was I had no self-worth, and I spent a lifetime managing low self-worth. Happiness and low self-worth don't go together. They are totally separate from each other.

Statistically, how many of the seven billion people living on earth have healthy self-worth? There have been many studies done, and the determination of most of those studies is there are far more people with low self-worth or no self-worth than there are people with healthy self-worth.

With regard to education, I can tell you firsthand, a child with healthy self-worth learns two to four times faster than a child with no self-worth. I created a list of 21 traits of self-worth, and at my presentations I would ask adult audiences all over the world to tell me two or three traits of healthy self-worth.

I was absolutely astounded that in huge audiences, there were very few people that could name one or two traits of healthy self-worth, much less half of them. That's why the divorce rate is sky-rocketing. That's why addiction is out of control. That's why death is out of control.

It's all related to self-worth. It's because there is nothing in a human being's life that is not related to self-worth. Self-worth is also a reason why a person cannot unconditionally love or be unconditionally loved. In the world of self-worth, love is conditional. There's nothing outside the realm of self-worth. Nothing. Implement The 21 Day Self Worth Challenge™, and thrive.

If you do not have self-worth, you will not be honest. If you do not have self-worth, you will not forgive yourself and other people. Why? It's because you consider yourself unworthy. You consider yourself not worthy of forgiveness, and think other people aren't worthy of being forgiven.

I want every human on the earth to know the elements of The Happiness Formula. It doesn't mean knowing the formula will force them to practice the formula. But if they know the formula, it gives them an option that they didn't have before they understood it.

I analyzed it all, and did thousands of hours of research. I used it with my closest friends. I applied it to my own life. I applied it to the relationships I've been in, in friendships and in work environments. I applied The Happiness Formula™ in every aspect of my life. I noticed that in nearly all the people I've crossed paths with; over 25 years in the personal development industry, and in 14 years as an international artist, almost everyone was missing either one or all three of the emotional foundation of a healthy, well lived life.

There is a global theory that sickness and disease has its origin in emotion. I made a determination through a tremendous amount of research that three things create what I call your emotional immune system.

1. My description is the human body has two immune systems: An emotional immune system and a physical immune system. The physical immune system takes it direction from the emotional immune system.

2. Adult life is based on the foundation of three things: A relationship foundation, a financial foundation, and a career to provide food, shelter and clothing.

3. The third part is your health. Relationships, finances and your health is the basis of a human life at the reality level. Those three things go back to the self-worth part of the formula.

The Happiness Formula™ is solid. It can be taught in any group of people: The corporate world, college institutions, and middle or elementary schools. I did that. I taught the formula to kindergarten and elementary grade children in a school in London. Any teacher, any presenter can teach it.

Five years ago, I had the Formula embroidered on a black baseball cap in gold lettering: The Happiness Formula F2HT2SW=HF10. Wherever I wore the cap, it always provoked questions, no matter where I was. I could be in a gas station, a college bookstore, a hospital, a school, a grocery store. The age group or gender didn't matter. I paid attention to how many people asked me passively, and how many people were fully engaged. I was looking for the marketing message.

I noticed immediately that no one was passive. I've had many people take out a piece of paper and a pen and write the Formula down, especially at colleges. I spoke every year for 12 years at UCSD, University of California San Diego to 300 teenagers from 25 countries, and taught the Formula to them. Most of the employees in all the campus stores are college students, and when I would walk into a coffee shop, the students would pause in their work, asking me to describe the Formula in detail as they wrote it down. This happened many times, and I equate that to those being establishments of higher learning. Those particular individuals are interested in learning (a) a formula and (b) something that has extreme substance. They saw profound substance in those three things.

It goes without saying that we're living in a time period with extreme emotional deprivation. I see it everywhere.

I tell people constantly it is never your circumstances that controls your destiny or your future. It is never your circumstances that control your happiness, never. It is only your choices.

Happiness depends upon ourselves.

–Aristotle

If you decide that happiness is something that is outside of you and if you think you can chase it, catch it, buy it, or sleep with it, to erase the situations that have caused you pain and suffering, that will not happen. The Happiness Formula™ gives you the ability to lead a balanced, well-lived life. It does not give you the ability to avoid pain and suffering. It gives you the balance to still live a well lived, healthy, happy, nurturing thriving life. It gives you the ability to be resilient. A life without resilience is not a life well lived.

People ask me why I don't mention gratitude or faith. Built into self-worth is courage, kindness, empathy, generosity, gratitude, faith, trust, resilience, and freedom.

Implementing The Happiness Formula™ gives you the ability to understand yourself and other people. You can look at people and rather than judge them, regardless of circumstances, you can find empathy in every situation. That leads to the last part of self-worth, unconditional love.

I routinely post daily on my Facebook page as way to stay in touch with my global community. One of the things I often post about is that love is one of the most misused, misrepresented words in the English language. It's just a word. Unconditional love is a well-balanced life. I recently read that only 0.04% of people on planet earth truly understand what unconditional love is and actually practice it. That means you can unconditionally love somebody who hates you, mistreats you, uses you, abuses you. You can still unconditionally love them. It does not mean that you allow them continue to harm you. But when you unconditionally love people, your heart will hurt. It's okay. Unconditional love is part of healthy self-worth. The word love is part of marginal self-worth, challenged self-worth or no self-worth. If you have no self-worth, love often is used to get somebody to love you back.

As we go through our life, we experience what we consider both positive and negative circumstances. Emotionally and physically, we typically act in accordance with our belief systems. The reality is, we can choose to feel any emotion even if the circumstances are negative. Suffering is a choice based on the way we filter our life situations. At any time, we can also give a positive meaning no matter what the situation. Happiness is an emotional response. Can you be happy if you are rejected? Absolutely! It is a choice. It is not mandated that we choose pain. You filter your emotions based on how you were conditioned, mainly as a child. Happiness is a by-product of emotional choices and healthy self-worth, not external short term gratification.

People who have read my book, The Happiness Formula™: The Ultimate Life Makeover have asked how I can be happy with all that has happened to me. It is because I know your circumstances do not control your emotions, or your future. Your choices do. I know what my purpose and my mission is. I don't have to search for it. I know what it is.

If you attempt to manage the outside world you will only frustrate yourself because you have no control over the outside world. Once you make the decision to manage your internal world, you will find that's where all happiness and success originates. The purpose of life is to give life meaning, and from the meaning you give it, you can create happiness and joy.

Happiness is not a destination. Happiness is a journey of life well lived. A life well lived is based on the foundation of virtue: forgiveness, honesty, truth and self-worth. All you have ever searched for lives inside of you right now. Look inside and you will find it after you clear the baggage from times past.

Your health, wealth, and happiness live inside your heart.

APPENDIX
ESSENTIAL AUTHORS
Featured in Nine Scrolls of Essential Wisdom

Dr. Wanda Krause

Wanda is a voice for success through redefining activism. She uses principles of spiritual activism as an integral way of being and so influencing change. It is Wanda's passion to assist people to act from one's core place of desire and guidance to take their lives to whole different levels of creativity and, therefore, to be effective leaders in this world-changing the world.

Bernice Angoh

Poet, author, thinker and humanitarian. Bernice is a transformational writer and speaker, Editorial director and Creative Liaison for Essential Wisdom LLC and contributor to Manifest Publishing LLC.

Dave Elliot

When it comes to helping people experience the love they truly deserve, Dave Elliott is a noted expert, author, product developer, international speaker and an accomplished coach who gets results for his clients all over the world. Whether he's sharing his expertise on some of today's most widely-read relationship websites or on TV, radio or stage, Dave's gift for relationship transformation will lead to the new awareness, skills and strategies to get the breakthrough results you really want and need.

Essential Authors

Dr. Jim Rogers

As a Relationship Consciousness Expert and Mentor™, Jim Rogers has been highly instrumental in helping save relationships, and marriages, as well as helping many find a deeper understanding of what it means to love themselves.

Dr. Nic Lucas

Dr. Nic has a unique skill set in business and personal growth with expertise in rapid mind and behavior change, leadership coaching, and health, fitness, and well-being. Nic's purpose is to enlighten and empower leaders and entrepreneurs to reach toward their dynamic potential, and in so doing he draws on his extensive background in health, research, business, influence and behavior change.

Penny Zenker

A productivity expert, strategic business coach, international speaker and trainer, radio personality, and author, Penny Zenker is also the creator of P10: Productivity Accelerator. Penny is an entrepreneur and innovator. She founded and later sold a multimillion dollar technology company where she established a solid brand and developed products that were recognized and sold internationally.

Shajen Joy Aziz

Shajen Joy Aziz holds master's degrees in both psychology and education. She is an award winning international best-selling author, educator, and documentary filmmaker. Her

Essential Authors

project Discover the Gift has been released in 22 countries and 12 languages and is now a globally recognized Life-Coaching Certification Program. A founding member of the Association of Transformational Leaders, Shajen Joy is an acclaimed speaker and educator with an extensive web presence and a devoted fan base. Her work has been featured in The Huffington Post, CNN, ABC, NBC, Spirit and Destiny Magazine, Examiner.com, Spiritual Networks, Life Connections, Vision Magazine, among many others.

Gary King

A speaker, author, and successful entrepreneur, Gary King understands happiness and shares life experiences and stories that defy logic. The Happiness Formula presentation is a culmination of efforts put into 25 years of research, reading 2,000 books on personal development, and working in the personal development industry for 24 years rubbing elbows with Anthony Robbins and similar presenters.

Dave Gould - CEO - Essential Wisdom LLC

A speaker and author Dave Gould is a master thought painter and thought artist, who is quickly rising in the ranks as a successful social entrepreneur. His innovative thinking focuses on bringing progressive ideas and new business models to the world; ideas that are grounded in personal development through fresh and transformative frontiers and avenues like never before.

Dave's background in the entertainment industry and creative productions include an exhaustive list of creative projects dating back to 1985 including, but not limited to, marketing, branding and business administration.

Throughout the years he has worked on several projects and businesses within the film production, theatrical and music industries.

Dave continuously expands known and specific variables within systems of creative expression and business models-- always seeking to re-engineer "the Box" and most of the times completely vanquishing it, a visionary thought leader and ultra-creative individual.

His newest company, Essential Wisdom LLC, is a media mindset and publishing group which sets itself apart from both traditional publishing models and self-publishing models. Essential Wisdom generates forward-thinking, progressive ideas on how the world should communicates ideas, share knowledge and educate the next generation of, those who already are or seeking to be, thinkers, innovators, entrepreneurs and game-changers.

ESSENTIAL WISDOM is a Mindset Group and Publisher. The Essential Wisdom brand is the creator of various subject multi author anthologies designed to empower and encourage readers to live their life in greatness and personal impact on the world around them.

EPILOGUE
ESSENTIAL WISDOM

We hope you have enjoyed these sample chapters from *Essential Wisdom: Personal Development and Soul Transformation*. This is but a very brief peek into our first book, project, brand and Essential Wisdom culture. We are living in the best of times and there's no better way to move forward than to move together. With your love, support and participation, we can effect the change we each desire; the kind of change that starts a new movement towards the evolution in the collective consciousness of mankind. We're extremely excited for you to read the full version of the book when it debuts later this year. Here is the list of the 33 chapters in the book:

Our Chapters:
1. *Your Awakening: A New Beginning*
2. *Birth: The Day We Chose Our Destiny—A Life of Potential* by Bernice Angoh
3. *Universal Law of Love: The Awakened Self* by Dr. Wanda Krause
4. *Dating: A New Kind Of Relationship, Seeking Self Aware Compatibility* by Roman Ramsey
5. *Relationship Exit Strategy: Healing When It's Over—Handling the End and Transition* by Dr. Jim Rogers
6. *Marriage: Creating an Awakened Legendary Relationship*

by Dave Elliot

7. **Children: Parenting In The Coming Age of Awakening–Raising Self Aware Children** by Dr. Joe Rubino
8. **Giving and Paying it Forward: The Gift of Presence—Giving Your Time Humble Service to Others**
9. **Healthy Living: Creating the New Body** by Tim Staggs
10. **Work: The New Success Story—Finding Your Passion, Identity, and Value** by James Woosley
11. **Personal Mastery: Mastering Your Master** by Barry Demp
12. **Joy and Sorrow: Emotional Health–The Balance** by Lise Lansue
13. **Home and Habitat: An Awakened Footprint** by E.J. Luu
14. **The Outer Self: Presenting Your Awareness to the World and Finding Your Voice** by Susanne Sulby
15. **MasterMinds: The Art of Negotiation and Winning Friends** by Dennis Thurman
16. **Laws & Activism: A Self-Awareness for Change** by Dr. Wanda Kraus
17. **Freedom: Overcoming Fears and Limitations to Achieve What Your Heart Desires** by Dave Albin
18. **Money: Developing Competence, Success Equations, and Empowerment** by Faith Dugan
19. **Reason and Passion: Finding and Living Your Passion and Purpose** by Billy J. Brown II
20. **Pain: Hard Lessons Learned—Functional vs. Dysfunctional Learning Processes** by Dave Gould
21. **Self Esteem: Stimulating Your Self Esteem Through Awareness** by Mike Markovski
22. **Self-Actualization: Your Spritual Spunk** by Shajen Joy Aziz
23. **Friendship: Bringing Awareness to Develop Relationships** by Vickie Smith
24. **Teaching: Value of Mentoring and Coaching** by Marc Mawhinney
25. **Choose to Step into Your Greatness** by Dr. Nic Lucas
26. **The Heart of Productivity: Maximizing Your Potentials—Developing Skills & Resources** by Penny Zenker
27. **The Art of Communication: Speaking Life** by Gary Barnes
28. **Time & Goals: Managing Your Greatest Asset** by T. Allen Hanes
29. **Good and Evil: Your Good Turns—Identifying and Overcoming Negative Influences** by Tim McAuley
30. **Prayer: Meditation and Thought Painting, LOA, Being Creative, Shattering the Limits** by Dave Gould

31. **Sacred Masculine/Feminine: Understanding Identity Roles We Each Carry—Awakening Our Complete Dual Soul** by Leilla Blackwell
32. **Pleasure: The New Forms of Freedoms and Deeper Physical Connections** by Debra Warshaw
33. **Gratitude: The Birth of Happiness** by Bernice Angoh
34. **Happiness Formula: Journey of a Life Well-Lived** by Gary King
35. **Religion and Spiritual Awareness: Finding Your Connectedness** by Tiffany Ayapana
36. **Death: What Can We Really Expect After Life (We Don't Die)** by Sandra Champlain
37. **The Farewell: Blessings On Your Awakening—Awaken to Your Transformation** by Dave Gould

SO IN CLOSING

We are finding that in the early discussions among influencers we have shared this project with, there is a consensus that this book really might become one of THE MOST GIFTED books ever.... people are seeing the real value of sharing impactful this information with friends co-workers and their loved ones... we would like to see our message become contagious... an epidemic...a global shift in mindset....it doesn't matter what your politics are... if you hold a particular religious belief, at what point you are in your financial and personal wealth desire... we think that it is a foundational human need to succeed and strive for happiness

So with that in mind we are offering a chance for you to purchase the book now at a special discounted price, we would like to offer you a chance to join in the fast growing movement of essential wisdom and giving you an incredible incentive to purchase an even more discounted book to give to those you love.

We are creating our global tribe and we want YOU to join. We can't begin to express the gratitude we have for you by purchasing our book now and sharing our message...it is you as early supporter that will help us take our message to the world.

Now that you have read 9 of the chapters will you help us do that?

Visit us @
www.essentialwisdom.com

www.ingramcontent.com/pod-product-compliance
Lightning Source LLC
LaVergne TN
LVHW051838080426
835512LV00018B/2956